Katherine Paterson

by Alice Cary

The Learning Works, Inc.
Santa Barbara, California

The Learning Works

Written by
Alice Cary

Edited by
Kimberley Clark

Page design and editorial production by
Clark Editorial & Design

Cover photo by
Beltrami's Photography

For Mom and Dad with love.
Many thanks to Katherine Paterson, to Kimberley Clark,
and to Debbie Bauman Rosenberg for her editorial savvy and advice.

The Learning Works, Inc.
P. O. Box 6187
Santa Barbara, CA 93160

Copyright © 1997—The Learning Works, Inc.
All rights reserved.

Library of Congress Cataloging-in-Publication Data:

Cary, Alice.
    Katherine Paterson / by Alice Cary.
        p.   cm. -- (The Learning Works meet the author series)
    "Books by Katherine Paterson": p. 134-135.
    Summary: Examines the life and writing career of the Newbery Award
-winning author of "The Bridge to Terabithia" and "Jacob Have I
Loved."
    ISBN 0-88160-281-7 (pbk.)
    1. Paterson, Katherine--Juvenile literature. 2. Women authors,
American--20th century--Biography--Juvenile literature.
3. Children's stories--Authorship--Juvenile literature.
[1. Paterson, Katherine. 2. Authors, American. 3. Women-
-Biography.]   I. Title.   II. Series.
PS3566.A779Z625 1997
813'.54--dc21
    [B]   97-668
                                                                CIP
                                                                AC

Printed in the United States of America.

Contents

Preface 5

Part One / Gypsy: Her Story 10

1   Spook Baby 12

2   Two Pairs of Chopsticks and Katherine 18

3   Incredible Journey 26

4   The Worst Day Ever 34

5   Back to China 40

6   War 47

7   Eye of the Hurricane 55

8   Where to Now? 61

Part Two / Finding Her Voice 73

9   Bridge to Adulthood 76

10 The Music of the East 83

11 Three Pairs of Chopsticks 91

12 Fifteen Minutes a Day 98

13 Matters of Life and Death 106

14 Vorin's Gift 115

15 Jacob Have I Wrestled 123

Afterward 129

Time Line 132

Books by Katherine Paterson 134

About the Author 136

John and Katherine with their granddaughters,
Katherine and Margaret, in 1994

Preface

Well, incredible as it seems, my life is based on a true story. Sometimes it seems incredible even to me ... but rarely does it have such a satisfying plot line.... Thus, in a real sense, I am constantly writing autobiography, but I have to turn it into fiction in order to give it credibility.

"The Story of My Lives"
The Spying Heart

One of Katherine Paterson's favorite fan letters is a note of few words:

Dear Mrs. Paterson,
    Thank you for the book, *The Great Gilly Hopkins*. I love the book. I am on page 16.
Your friend
Always
Eddie Young

Like Eddie, anyone who opens a book by Katherine Paterson—whether it's *The Great Gilly Hopkins, Bridge to Terabithia, Jacob Have I Loved, Lyddie,* or any of her other novels and picture books—immediately realizes that this is a *good book*, a special story from start to finish. Many people consider Katherine Paterson to be one of the best children's authors writing today.

Strangely, she never meant to be a writer, and she's still not completely sure why she became one. Katherine Womeldorf Paterson was well past her thirtieth birthday before realizing that she *was* a writer, and that writing was exactly what she wanted to do.

Still, she didn't become an author completely by accident. She wrote stories and plays as a child, and she always loved books. In addition, she comes from a family of storytellers. Both of Katherine's parents grew up in the South, where Katherine spent part of her childhood, and where people pride themselves on the art of spinning tales. She's even a distant relation of Samuel Clemens, better known as Mark Twain; her middle name is Clements, a variation of the surname.

Perhaps what really started her on her way to becoming a writer was the fact that her parents were missionaries, people who help others and teach them about religion. The job requires talking and telling stories, and it meant that the family traveled the world and had extraordinary adventures.

There are "famous stories," as Katherine calls them, about every member of the Womeldorf family. Many star Katherine, such as the story about the time she got lost in Hong Kong, or the time she and her sister were nearly trampled by Japanese soldiers.

Difficult as it is to choose a place to begin the story of Katherine Paterson's life, perhaps it makes sense to start in a cathedral in France, before she was born. Every tale needs a hero, and Katherine's first, and perhaps greatest, was her father, George Raymond Womeldorf.

As World War I raged in Europe, so many men were injured that French cathedrals were used as temporary hospitals. In one cathedral lay a young American soldier, Raymond Womeldorf, gravely wounded by shrapnel and a victim of poisonous gas. He had crossed the Atlantic to drive an ambulance for French troops, as did many men of his generation, including the famous writer Ernest Hemingway.

A French doctor stopped to look at the patient. After a quick glance and a pinch of the man's toe, he shook his head and said, "This fellow's gone. Forget about him."

But Raymond was far from gone. Not only was he conscious, he spoke French and understood that the doctor was abandoning him. He frantically tried to move something—anything. Finally he managed to wiggle a toe, then struggled to whisper a few words, demanding to be taken to an American hospital.

He eventually lost his right leg to gangrene, but he returned home to the United States alive. During the long months of recovery that followed, he became a patient at Walter Reed Medical Center in Washington, D.C., where a wealthy woman named Mrs. Brown periodically visited the wards, trying to cheer up the courageous patients.

She took an instant liking to Raymond Womeldorf, an unusually friendly and intelligent young man. She realized that he needed a change of scenery, so she sent him and several other patients for further recuperation on her family estate on Long Island, New York.

After many months Raymond Womeldorf recovered from his injuries. He decided to attend the seminary, a school for the study of religion. One day, while traveling on a streetcar, he met a student named Mary Goetchius, from Georgia, who attended the school for women. They began dating and were married in June 1923. Later that summer they sailed for China. After spending two years learning the country's language, they moved to the Chinese countryside to do missionary work for the Presbyterian Church.

Here's where Katherine enters the story. Raymond and Mary had five children; Katherine Clements Womeldorf was their middle child, born in northeastern China in 1932. As she grew older, she admired her father so much that she sometimes walked behind him, carefully imitating the slight limp caused by his artificial leg.

Meanwhile, oceans away, Mrs. Brown stayed in touch with the brave young soldier and his family, even visiting them overseas. She also sent them books from time to time, since there were no English libraries or bookstores in China. Everyone—especially Katherine—looked forward to the packages containing beautiful new books from half-way around the world.

Now, years later, the books Katherine has written are read all over the world. If you were to meet her, you would see a woman brimming with laughter, compassion, and, most of all, stories. Ask a few questions about her life, and at first she's apt to reply slowly, somewhat reluctantly. But one tale soon leads to another, and—if you're lucky—another and another.

In that one tale about her father's recovery from his war injuries are several elements that appear over and over again, both in Paterson's life and in her books—danger, courage, friendship, loneliness, and, as Katherine Paterson puts it, "one heart in hiding reaching out to another."

People, stories, and words reaching out—such is the essence of Katherine Paterson's life—whether it's her father trying to signal that he's alive, a wealthy woman befriending him and later sending books to his children, a shy little girl listening to her mother read, or, years later, millions of readers turning the pages of Katherine Paterson's novels.

In an essay called "Heart in Hiding," Katherine Paterson explains what writers do: "We are trying to communicate that which lies in our deepest heart, which has no words, which can only be hinted at through the means of a story. And somehow, miraculously, a story that comes from deep in my heart calls from a reader that which is deepest in his or her heart, and together from our secret hidden selves we create a story that neither of us could have told alone."

Here are some of the true-life stories that fill Katherine Paterson's heart.

Part I
Gypsy: Her Story

Jip: His Story is Katherine Paterson's novel about a boy in the 1850s who tumbles off a wagon and is left behind by his family. He is called Jip because townsfolk speculate that his parents must have been gypsies.

Katherine also came from a family of wanderers. By the time she turned eighteen, the Womeldorfs had moved more than fifteen times. She was taught that wandering was part of her heritage. The stories that have influenced her most are the stories of the Bible, especially that of Abraham, whom God commanded to leave home and seek out a new land. His story is known the world over; this nomadic leader is revered in three religions: Christianity, Judaism, and Islam.

Along with wandering, the theme of longing and searching for a parent is central to Katherine's writing. In her first novel, *The Sign of the Chrysanthemum*, a twelfth-century Japanese boy named Muna desperately searches for his father, a noble warrior. Katherine explores the issue again and again, whether through Jiro trying to find his parents in the midst of riots (*The Master Puppeteer*); Gilly scheming to be rescued by her mother (*The Great Gilly Hopkins*); Park trying to learn about his father who died in Vietnam (*Park's Quest*); Lyddie Worthen being abandoned by her parents and forced to work in the mills of Lowell, Massachusetts (*Lyddie)*; Vinnie Matthews mourning the death of her father (*Flip-Flop Girl)*; or Jip.

In an essay called "The Story of My Lives," Paterson explains what happens in each of her books:

> *The hero must leave home, confront fabulous dangers, and return the victor to grant boons to his fellows. Or a wandering nobody must go out from bondage through the wilderness and by the grace of God become truly someone who can give back something of what she has been given.*

In a way, this is just what happened to Katherine.

Chapter 1
Spook Baby

Finally, she smiled at Lizzie. "Isn't she lovely," she said. "What charming freckles." Then she turned and stared at me again. "Now Mary," she said, "you can't tell me this one belongs to you. She doesn't look like the rest of the family." She laughed as though she had said something funny. "Where on earth did you pick up this little stranger?"

"Why I Never Ran Away from Home"
When I Was Your Age: Original Stories About Growing Up

Just the thought of steamed pork dumplings was enough to make Katherine's mouth water. Those tender pillows of dough wrapped around juicy minced pork were pure heaven as far as she was concerned.

Sometimes her parents took her to buy dumplings from the peddlers' carts in Huaian, the Chinese city where she spent her early years. She loved to stroll on top of the ancient walls surrounding Huaian, gazing at the sights below and drinking in the sounds and smells.

The blonde, curly-haired American girl didn't realize she was a foreigner. To her, China—a vast country full of rice fields, bamboo groves, and mountains—was home. The United States was nothing more than some faraway land her parents often discussed, as magical and mythical as Oz.

The Womeldorfs lived with other Chinese families inside the gates of a school for boys, where Mr. Womeldorf was the principal.

Their home was Chinese-style with a low, flat pagoda roof. It wasn't heated until the Womeldorfs installed a large, coal-burning stove to provide warmth during the long winters.

Outside was a vegetable garden where Katherine enjoyed helping her father. Once the asparagus seeds were planted, she liked to be the first to spot the green shoots breaking through the soil. The family had several pets, including rabbits as well as goats, which provided milk. For fun, Mr. Womeldorf designed a simple merry-go-round for his children, which a Chinese carpenter built in the backyard. Katherine didn't have to go far to enjoy herself.

As missionaries, the Womeldorfs didn't have much money, but they had servants, as was the custom at the time. There was a nurse, called an *amah*, who helped tend to the children: Katherine; her baby sister, Helen; her older sister, Lizzie (Elizabeth); and Sonny (Raymond), the oldest. Another brother, Charles, was born a year after Sonny, but he died when he was only a few weeks old.

A cook prepared Chinese meals, which Katherine and her family ate with chopsticks. They switched to knives and forks whenever Mrs. Womeldorf got out her *Fannie Farmer Cookbook* and told the cook how to prepare American dishes.

Katherine's father wasn't home for dinner very often. As a missionary, he and his best friend, a Chinese man named Mr. Lee, were away for weeks at a time. They rode donkeys along cart paths from village to village, taking food and medicine to hungry and sick people and telling them about the Christian religion.

Katherine always missed her father terribly during these trips, but she didn't like to complain because she knew how much he enjoyed helping the villagers. She loved to hear about his adventures, how he and Mr. Lee sometimes slept in pigsties because farmers had no other beds to offer them. Those stories left Katherine scratching at imaginary flea bites; her father described the nights with such detail that she couldn't help feeling itchy.

Mrs. Womeldorf also told stories, reading aloud in her soft Georgia accent from *The Wind in the Willows*, *The Tale of Peter Rabbit*, *The Jungle Book*, and fairy tales by the Grimm Brothers and Hans Christian Andersen. Katherine snuggled as close as she could and inhaled deeply, holding her teddy bear and breathing in her mother's sweet lavender scent.

Since there were no bookstores or libraries for westerners, some books came from her parents' friend, Mrs. Brown, and others were gifts from their many British friends, who were also missionaries. Often Katherine begged her mother to read *East o' the Sun and West o' the Moon*, a Norwegian folk tale so exciting that the mere mention of the title was enough to send shivers down her spine.

Sometimes Mrs. Womeldorf also taught her children

lessons. Because there was no English school, Mrs. Womeldorf taught from the same book she had used in kindergarten, a book called *Jo Boy*, which her former teacher had sent to China. It was filled with activities and stories about a young hero named Jo Boy, a character Katherine never forgot, although few people outside of her family have ever heard of him.

More familiar is one of Katherine's favorite stories, "In Which Eeyore Has a Birthday and Gets Two Presents." What a wonderful tale she thought it was, with Winnie-the-Pooh and his friends trying so hard to make the day special for the sad old donkey. In the end Eeyore is happy even after everything goes wrong. Katherine felt a little like Eeyore on her fourth birthday. Because she was born on Halloween, Sonny, age eight, and Lizzie, nearly six, called her "Spook Baby."

"Am not," Katherine would cry, tears streaming down her cheeks. "I'm not a spook and I'm not a baby."

Sometimes, though, she wondered exactly who she was. She wasn't the baby anymore, she wasn't the oldest, and, in some ways, she felt she looked different from her brother and sisters. She longed for Lizzie's freckles and good looks; strangers sometimes stopped to say how beautiful Lizzie was.

On the day Katherine turned four, Mrs. Womeldorf had some errands to run. Katherine, Lizzie, and Sonny rode with her through the streets of Huaian in a *ricksha*, a two-wheeled carriage pulled by a ricksha man.

As Katherine sat on her mother's lap, she noticed that today Huaian was festooned with flags and banners. Too young to understand Chinese politics, she didn't realize that a man named Chiang Kai-shek, the leader of this part of

China, was also celebrating a birthday. All of the shops were decorated in his honor, all of them, that is, except for one small, deserted shop.

"Look over there," Katherine said, pointing, her voice filled with disapproval. "They don't know it's my birthday."

Sonny and Lizzie began to howl. "Don't you know anything, Spook Baby?" Sonny taunted. "Those flags aren't for you."

"Nobody but us knows it's your birthday," Lizzie added.

"They don't even know it's Halloween," Sonny said.

Sonny was right—here in China, Halloween wasn't a holiday. Nobody wore costumes or went trick-or-treating. Katherine had never seen a pumpkin.

"Today's still your special day, Katherine," Mrs. Womeldorf said.

Katherine managed a smile, thinking about the fun she knew was in store. As a substitute for pumpkins, her mother had pasted faces cut from black construction paper onto persimmons, small orange-colored fruit. She had also made mango ice cream, orange like the tropical fruit from which it is made. But the best pumpkin of all would be her cake, shaped like a jack-o-lantern's face.

Yes, Katherine thought, today would be wonderful.

Katherine's first playmates were her brother, sisters, and the Chinese children who lived nearby. Her best friend of all was Mrs. Loo, their neighbor, who taught Bible classes and reading. She wasn't married and lived alone, so she was always glad to see Katherine, who often joined her for lunch.

One day, when Katherine told her mother where she

was going, Mrs. Womeldorf smiled and said, "Katherine, if you keep eating so much Chinese food, you're going to turn into a Chinese girl."

Could that really happen? Katherine wondered. She ran to peer in a mirror and saw that she looked the same as she always had. Just then her stomach growled, so she hurried over to see Mrs. Loo.

Katherine greeted her friend by speaking Chinese. The Womeldorfs spoke English but used Chinese when talking to natives. Mrs. Womeldorf marveled that her children somehow knew when to use Chinese and when to use English, and never got confused.

Mrs. Loo hugged Katherine and told her to go wash her hands. Katherine did as she was told, but she was distracted by the bucket of water that had been carried inside from the Grand Canal, an ancient waterway more than 1,000 miles long—the world's longest canal. She played in the water for several minutes, until she suddenly noticed her fingers, which had wrinkled like prunes. *What was wrong?* she wondered with alarm. *Are my fingers going to fall off? Am I sick?*

Sobbing, she ran to Mrs. Loo. Too upset to speak, she held up her hands.

"What happened?" Mrs. Loo asked, her face filled with concern. She examined Katherine's hands carefully, then gave them a squeeze, saying, "Don't worry. The cold water did this. Soon your fingers will be smooth, good as new."

Katherine smiled. Mrs. Loo knew how to make everything right. But Katherine's peaceful world of Mrs. Loo's lunches, steamed dumplings, and Daddy's merry-go-round would soon be turned upside down.

Chapter 2
Two Pairs of Chopsticks
and Katherine

"Until I was nearly five I had a very happy childhood. I loved my home and my family and the Chinese and Europeans I knew. . . . But once the war began, life began to be scary and harrowing."
interview with Katherine Paterson (spring 1996)

The Womeldorfs' vacation had started out wonderfully. But now Katherine felt everything had been ruined. How could things change so quickly?

Because summers were always hot in Huaian, in the summer of 1937, the Womeldorfs traveled south to the resort town of Kuling, high in the mountains where the weather would be cooler.

They went by train from Huaian, then took a very different kind of ride up to Kuling. Because the terrain was too steep for trains or rickshas, tourists were carried up the mountain by chair—basically, a ricksha without wheels. Steps had been built into the mountainside, which rose nearly straight up. Katherine didn't dare look, much less move, as she and her family were carried by "bearers," two men in front of each chair and two behind. Only a few feet and bushes separated them from the mountain's cliff-like edge.

Once in Kuling, Katherine spent as much time as possible in the swimming pool. She couldn't stay underwater as long as Lizzie or go in the deep end like Sonny, but she loved to splash and play, and she was determined to learn how to swim.

Her parents, however, had other things on their minds. Mrs. Womeldorf was expecting another baby in August. She tired easily, and Helen, who was just over a year old, required a lot of attention. The amah had accompanied the family to Kuling, but even with her help, Mrs. Womeldorf had her hands full.

Something else was worrying Katherine's parents: politics. Chiang Kai-shek ruled part of the country, but he was being challenged by another leader named Mao Tse-tung. Mao wanted China to become a Communist country in which workers would own and manage the land and factories.

To further complicate matters, Japan also wanted to control China. In 1931, Japanese soldiers had invaded Manchuria, an economically important region in the northeast. Then, in July 1937, Japanese forces attacked central China. For a while, Chiang Kai-shek and Mao Tse-tung stopped fighting each other to fend off their common enemy, the Japanese.

Although Katherine knew none of these details, soon she and her family were affected. One evening they heard airplanes overhead. As the noise of the droning engines grew louder, Mr. and Mrs. Womeldorf jumped up and put out the lights.

"What's going on?" Sonny's voice sounded far away in the dark.

"Come here," Mr. Womeldorf ordered. "We need to sit together."

Katherine made her way to her father's lap. Lizzie and Sonny sat on each side of them, and Mrs. Womeldorf held Helen.

"This is an air raid," Mr. Womeldorf explained.

There was so much rumbling that Katherine imagined the entire sky must be full of planes. But she was too scared to open her eyes, much less look outside, which wouldn't have been allowed anyway.

"Whose planes are those?" Sonny asked.

"They're Japanese planes," Mr. Womeldorf replied.

Suddenly the rumbling turned into a series of loud, crackling *booms*, like a wild, terrifying thunderstorm. But this wasn't thunder; these were bombs. Katherine held her ears and buried her head in her father's chest, trying to make the noise disappear.

For what seemed like hours, the Womeldorfs sat— waiting, listening, and praying. Eventually the raid ended, and everyone tried to go to sleep. Katherine couldn't. She was afraid the planes would return.

They did. Not that night, but other nights, dropping bombs throughout the region. Katherine missed Mrs. Loo and their home in Huaian. And she missed her teddy bear, which somehow had been left behind.

One morning, the day after an air raid, Katherine was allowed to accompany her father to a village that had been bombed. People had been killed and many houses had been destroyed. Katherine held her father's hand as tightly as she could. Mr. Womeldorf was very quiet. He picked up a piece of debris and shook his head in disbelief.

"The shrapnel in these bombs was made in the United States," he said. "Our own country is helping to kill Chinese people—our friends."

"But Daddy, I thought Japanese soldiers dropped these bombs."

"They did, Katherine. But the metal was made in America, then sold to Japan."

Katherine wasn't sure what to make of all this. One thing she did know, however: she had never seen her father look so sad.

Although the family remained safe from Japanese attacks, something else happened that, to Katherine, felt like a bomb. In August, her youngest sister, Anne, was born.

Suddenly, in little more than a year, Katherine had not one, but two, baby sisters. For several years she had been the youngest in the family, until Helen came along. That had been bad enough, but now her mother was busier than ever, and Katherine felt lost and outnumbered.

Someone once commented to Mr. and Mrs. Womeldorf that now they had two pairs of chopsticks—and Katherine. First came Lizzie and Sonny, born close together, and now, Helen and Anne. Two perfect pairs.

It just isn't fair, Katherine told herself. *What does that make me? A leftover?*

One day Katherine saw her father packing his suitcase. "Are we going home, Daddy?" she asked. "I can't wait to get back to Huaian."

Mr. Womeldorf explained that he would be returning alone. There was work to be done at the school and at several small churches he had established in the countryside. Some of the people he knew needed food and medicine.

"But why can't we go? Maybe we could help you."

Mr. Womeldorf explained that because of the war, travel was too risky for the rest of the family. Between Kuling and Huaian were two armies, one from Japan and one from China, along with bandits and renegade soldiers. He assured Katherine that he would be very careful and that he would be back.

"Your job is to be brave, sweet girl" he told Katherine, "and to help your mother." "Sweet girl" was Mr. Womeldorf's pet name for each of his four daughters.

How could she help her mother? Katherine wondered. Lizzie already did all the helping. Even though Katherine knew how much her parents loved her, sometimes she needed her own chopstick.

"Daddy," Katherine said. "Could you do something for me? Could you bring me back my teddy bear?"

Mr. Womeldorf gave her a hug and promised to try to find her bear.

Not long after her father left, Katherine started kindergarten. There were enough other missionary children in Kuling to have a school. Soon, however, Katherine was ready to quit.

"What's wrong, dear?" her mother asked.

"The teacher is mean."

"She seems nice to me."

"Well, she isn't. She doesn't like me."

Her teacher was disappointed because Katherine didn't know how to cut with scissors. She tried and tried, but couldn't get it right. Either her hand would slip or the paper would slip just when she was ready to make a perfect, straight cut. Katherine was a flop at cutting and, it seemed, at everything else the teacher expected her to do.

Nighttime was no better. Every evening Katherine lay in bed and worried about her father. He couldn't call, since there weren't any telephones in the area, and they hadn't heard from him, not even a letter.

Where is he? Katherine wondered. *Is he safe? Is he alive?* He might not be—she had heard Sonny and his friends talk about soldiers, warlords, and bandits.

Don't be silly, she reassured herself. Her father knew how to deal with wars. He had already been through one in France. He had lost his leg, but he had survived.

As Katherine returned home from school one afternoon, she walked inside the door and found her father talking with her mother.

"Daddy!" she screamed, running to hug him.

Mr. Womeldorf reached down and lifted Katherine high in the air, peering at her closely through his glasses.

Katherine stared back. His clothes were rumpled and he looked tired, but, other than that, he looked just the same as always—handsome and strong.

"The bandits didn't get you?" she asked.

He shook his head, smiling slightly. "And *you*. Such a big girl now. I hear you've started kindergarten."

Katherine couldn't help herself—she frowned. She still

didn't like kindergarten, although at least she was used to it. But since she didn't want her father to think she was a sourpuss, she changed the subject and said, "I'm in the choir, too!"

Christmas was coming, and the missionary families had decided to form a children's choir. Katherine was *very* proud to belong. She felt grown up. As soon as the music started, all her worries seemed to fall away—bandits, bombs, baby sisters, and those confounded scissors.

As Christmas got closer, Katherine sang all the time. Her parents had assured her that Santa Claus knew they were in Kuling, not Huaian. And she had been good. At least she had tried, very, very hard, even if her kindergarten teacher didn't agree.

Finally, Christmas arrived. All of the foreign families gathered together for the concert. Katherine sang her heart out. The best part was when they sang her favorite carol, called "There's a Song in the Air." Ever since they had started rehearsing for the concert, the words had given her tremendous comfort. Often, when she felt lonely and scared, she sang them to herself. The world didn't seem like such a dangerous place when she sang:

There's a song in the air and a star in the sky,
There's a mother's deep prayer and a baby's low cry,
And the star rains its fire while the beautiful sing,
For the manger of Bethlehem cradles a king.

In the light of that star til the ages impearled,
And that song from afar has swept over the world,
Every hearth is aflame and the beautiful sing,
In the homes of the nations that Jesus is king.

When the applause came, Katherine felt like an angel—well, almost.

There was also a sparkling Christmas tree, and Santa himself was there, handing out presents. As she stood in line waiting her turn to talk to Santa, Katherine scrutinized all the presents under the tree. She knew which one must be hers: a beautiful doll with long shiny hair. She had never had a gorgeous doll like that. Now she could tend her baby while her mother and Lizzie looked after Helen and Anne. Maybe all the bad things that had happened the previous year had simply been a test of her goodness, and now she had passed with flying colors. Katherine plunked herself on Santa's knee, barely able to sit still.

"Ho, ho, ho," he chortled. "Why it's Katherine Womeldorf. Have you been a good little girl?"

She nodded, closed her eyes, and held out her hands. Santa reached over and handed her—a harmonica.

Katherine looked down in horror. The shiny instrument might as well have been a lump of coal. "Thank you," she mumbled, trying to hold back her tears.

That night Katherine lay in bed, not daring to think about who might have gotten that doll, some other girl who could cut well with scissors and do everything the teacher wanted.

Instead, she thought about her teddy bear, which her father hadn't been able to find. *Where is my bear? Did a Japanese soldier find him and take him home? Is some other child holding him this very minute?*

No, Katherine decided. Her teddy bear must be hidden somewhere in Huaian, tucked out of sight where her father hadn't looked. She hoped she could go home soon and find him.

Chapter 3
Incredible Journey

I have discovered as I have gone out into the world that most people do not regard missionary work as a respectable occupation. And I'm sure that many of us "mish kids" would argue whether having been born one was a plus or minus for the living of this life. There is no way to escape a certain peculiarity of personality.

"Sounds in the Heart"
The Spying Heart

Katherine never got a chance to look for her teddy bear. Early in the new year she and her family left Kuling. But instead of returning to Huaian, they were going to America. The journey would take a long time, requiring travel by chair down the mountains from Kuling, by train to Hong Kong, and, finally, by two different ships to the States.

The Presbyterian Mission Board had ordered the Womeldorfs to leave China, saying the country had become too dangerous. Even without the war, though, they would have left. They were almost due for a furlough—a periodic break, a chance for missionary families to return to their own country.

The three younger Womeldorf children had never been to America. Katherine was happy to leave the bombings behind. Her Chinese friends had told her wonderful stories about the United States, describing it as a fabulous kingdom where everyone was rich.

While her family fled to safety, for some reason disaster seemed to follow Katherine every step of the way.

Like the Womeldorfs, many foreign families vacationing in Kuling had been trapped by the war. Soon after the Christmas of 1937, a train arrived at the foot of the mountains to allow foreigners to evacuate. Large red crosses were painted on top of the train, a signal that soldiers should spare it from their bombs. The trip took a week. The train was crowded and there was no place to bathe. Katherine and her family slept in tiny bunks that lined the aisles.

One night Mr. Womeldorf was awakened by a loud *thump*! He looked down into the aisle and saw Katherine lying on her back, looking dazed.

"Are you all right?" he asked, jumping down to her side.

"My head hurts, Daddy." She rubbed it gingerly.

After examining her scalp, Mr. Womeldorf decided to consult his wife. He turned to waken her, but when he glanced back, the aisle was empty.

Where's Katherine? he wondered, beginning to panic. He

looked along the aisle, then checked her bunk. Thankfully, there she was, sound asleep.

Her father knew she must not have been hurt badly, but he feared she might fall again. Mr. Womeldorf conducted a quick search and found a rope, which he tied in crisscross fashion to make a net to catch Katherine if she should roll out.

When Katherine opened her eyes the next morning, she felt like she was in a cage. She didn't remember the previous night's fall.

"Daddy," she called out. "Help!"

Sonny and Lizzie got there first and started to laugh. For years afterward, whenever Katherine got confused about something, they teased her, saying, "When you fell out of that bunk, Katherine, something happened to your head!"

Finally the train pulled into Hong Kong, where thousands of refugees were pouring in from across the country. The Womeldorfs and other passengers from Kuling were taken to an elegant, old hotel. No rooms were left, forcing everyone to crowd into the lobby and sit on top of their luggage until other arrangements could be made.

Mr. Womeldorf went out to the streets to search for a place to stay until their ship departed. Dirty, hungry, and tired, the rest of the family huddled together, waiting.

Well-dressed men and women staying at the hotel came and went. Katherine noticed many of them staring at the weary travelers, frowning as though they were looking at criminals.

"What's wrong, Momma?" she asked. "Why don't they like us?"

Mrs. Womeldorf stared back at the gawkers, narrowing her eyes. "They're upset because we're making a mess of their pretty lobby." She sighed. "Don't they understand that we don't *like* being dirty? That we don't have a choice?"

From that moment, Mrs. Womeldorf taught her children to respect and sympathize with any and all refugees, and to remember that their own lives had once been altered by politics and war.

Mr. Womeldorf's hunt for lodging was successful. He returned and led his family to a room in a missionary residence where the seven of them could stay. It was crowded with cots, leaving no place to walk. Mr. Womeldorf took Katherine, Lizzie, and Sonny window-shopping while Mrs. Womeldorf tended to the babies.

Hong Kong was a bustling place. Legs and waists—that was all Katherine saw as she squeezed her father's hand tightly. People pushed, pulled, and shoved in every direction. Katherine had never been in such a crowded, busy city. There were noises, smells, and shops filled with toys, clothes, trinkets, and food—everything a person could want. In one shop a shiny ring caught her eye. She dropped her father's hand to look more closely. It was beautiful, and she wanted to make sure her father saw it. When she turned to tug at his coat, he was gone.

Katherine looked around. She saw more legs and waists, none of them belonging to her family. She was alone.

Panicking, she calmed herself by thinking they must have gone to the next shop. No problem. She was proud of herself for knowing what to do. But after shoving her way through the crowds to the next store, she had no luck. They weren't there. Or in the next shop. Or the next.

Katherine tried to retrace her steps to the first shop.

Maybe they were there waiting. But try as she might, she couldn't find the shop. She stopped on the sidewalk, the horror sinking in. She was lost.

Katherine sank to her knees and began to sob. How would her family ever find her in this huge, busy place?

"What's wrong?" someone asked, placing a hand gently on her shoulder.

Katherine looked up into the kind eyes of a woman—an Englishwoman, with the familiar accent of her parents' British friends. Katherine was crying so hard, it took several sobs and sniffs to answer.

"I'm l-l-lost," she finally answered.

"I see," the woman said gently, as if this were no cause for alarm. "Where do you live?"

Katherine stared. She wasn't sure. Should she say Kuling, or Huaian—or, perhaps, America? She didn't really live anywhere, not at the moment.

And then she remembered. Before her father had taken them out that day, her mother had taught her, Sonny, and Lizzie the address of the missionary residence.

Katherine carefully repeated the information, and her new friend smiled.

"Why then, I'll take you home. I know where that is."

She extended her hand, and Katherine held on as though clinging to a life raft. Before long they stood in front of the door to the Womeldorfs' room.

Her mother answered the door, holding Anne, with Helen at her heels. She looked at the British woman with surprise. Her jaw dropped the minute she saw Katherine.

"She was lost," the kind stranger explained.

"But, but—" Mrs. Womeldorf stammered, thoroughly confused. "She has a father. She was with him. Where is he?"

The woman quickly offered to go find him.

Mrs. Womeldorf described him, Lizzie, and Sonny.

Westerners were fairly easy to spot in Hong Kong, and the Englishwoman found Mr. Womeldorf searching for Katherine near the spot where she had found her sobbing. "Your daughter is safe with your wife," she told him. After he thanked her profusely, Katherine's guardian angel disappeared into the crowded Hong Kong streets.

Katherine never forgot the terror she felt that day. Even now, as an adult, when she arrives in a bustling foreign city, she is momentarily gripped with fear. The anxiety soon passes and Katherine nods, thinking: there it is again—the Hong Kong Syndrome.

Life seemed more normal once the Womeldorfs boarded the boat to America—a large German ship that was the first available passage to safety. Everyone settled into the family's cabin, not minding its small size since, by now, they were used to being jammed together.

They voyaged west, by way of Europe. Because of the war, the more direct, eastern route—across the Pacific Ocean toward California—wasn't safe.

Despite the additional days at sea, the detour had its advantages. Whenever the ship docked at a port that had a zoo, Mr. Womeldorf took the older children for a visit. In the Dutch East Indies (now called Indonesia), Katherine saw Dutch flags flying everywhere in celebration of the birth of the Dutch crown princess, Beatrix, who would one day become queen of the Netherlands. On the island of Ceylon (now called Sri Lanka) near the southern tip of India, Katherine was spellbound by a snake charmer.

Life onboard was not so adventurous. The ship's German crew seemed stern to Katherine; the atmosphere was formal. Because children weren't allowed to eat with adults, a steward presided over the young Womeldorfs while their parents ate in the dining room.

Aside from steamed dumplings, five-year-old Katherine wasn't interested in many foods. Worst of all was the pudding, which Katherine prodded and poked with her fork, pretending to eat.

The steward wasn't fooled. "Kat-rin-a, my dear," she would say, her voice gathering steam, "EAT YOUR PUD-DINK!"

The one place Katherine felt she could escape was the ship's swimming pool. Here, too, however, near-catastrophe struck. Katherine still couldn't swim, but she loved to hold onto the ladder and kick. One day her hands slipped and she went under, nearly drowning, until a twelve-year-old girl in the pool dragged her to safety. With great relief, Mrs. Womeldorf, who had been at the side of the pool watching Helen and Anne, dried Katherine off and led her children back to the cabin.

On the way, Katherine noticed a large photograph of a man on a wall. When she asked who it was, her mother frowned and told her it was Adolf Hitler, the leader of Germany. Katherine didn't realize it then, but even worse times were ahead, not just for her, but for the world.

In Southampton, England, the Womeldorfs changed ships. Before the last leg of their voyage, they spent several days in London, visiting sights such as Buckingham Palace and Westminster Abbey. But there were frightening places as well. Some of the figures in Madame Tussaud's famous wax museum made Katherine feel like screaming, and she *did* scream all the way across London Bridge, convinced that it was falling down.

Finally, after boarding the second ship and crossing the Atlantic, the long journey ended. Like so many refugees and immigrants, Katherine's first view of the United States was the Statue of Liberty, with her crowned head and welcoming torch held high. Katherine was thrilled at the thought of all the new, exciting things in store.

Chapter 4
The Worst Day Ever

Most of you who have moved to a new neighborhood and gone to a new school may remember a time when you were nobody. If people spoke to you, they did it in a superior "since-you-don't-even-know-where-the-lunchroom-is-I-will-be-very-kind-and-show-you" tone of voice. But most of the time you were ignored.

In one way or another, all of us understand the feeling of being out of it—of being treated as inferior, as invisible, as disposable, or, at any rate, as not fully deserving of respect.

Who Am I?

Katherine's Chinese friends had told her everything would be perfect in America, but perfect was just about the *last* word she would use to describe her new home.

Perhaps part of the problem was that it wasn't home and was never meant to be. The Womeldorfs were just dropping in for an extended visit, waiting to hear that China was safe enough for them to return. As they waited, they moved from place to place.

There were many American customs to learn, but Katherine was so young she remembers only a few details and impressions. At her age, the main challenge was trying to get used to school, which made moving and changing schools especially tough.

The family's first stop was the town of Lynchburg, Virginia, home of Mrs. Womeldorf's older sister, Aunt Anne. The household was exactly what Katherine needed after the long, eventful journey from Kuling—after falling out of bed on the train, getting lost in Hong Kong, and nearly drowning aboard the German ship.

Katherine adored her aunt. She made her feel at home in this strange new place, as did Uncle Ernest, a Southern Baptist minister. Their three children, older than Katherine, were kindhearted cousins who went out of their way to show the newcomers what they needed to know. If others had been as welcoming and comfortable as Aunt Anne's family, Katherine would have loved America.

But she didn't love it. Katherine was sent to kindergarten, which wasn't any better than school in Kuling. The teacher scared her. Katherine felt sure the woman didn't like her. Katherine wanted to please her, but, as hard as she tried, she couldn't figure out how.

Once school finally ended, the Womeldorfs left Aunt Anne's. Her parents worked for the missionary board, which required some travel. They frequently went from church to church to talk about their work in China. As a result, the Womeldorfs left their children to spend much of the summer in Lexington, Virginia, on the farm where Mr. Womeldorf had grown up. Katherine's father wanted his children to get to know his side of the family and to live in the same place he had loved as a boy.

Such a summer might have been enchanting, but it wasn't. Katherine was miserably homesick for her parents, for Huaian, and for China. Whenever possible, she hid in the springhouse, where she acted out stories, both imagined and from books. She also felt comforted by the animals, bees, flowers, and the many wonderful scents in the air.

Grandmother Womeldorf, a widow, was a petite yet tireless woman who managed both the farm and the family. She had nine children, only two of whom (Katherine's father and one of his brothers) had left the farm. This meant that there were plenty of adults to keep a strict eye on the young, energetic Womeldorf brood.

In the fall of 1938, Katherine's parents returned and moved the family to a missionary apartment in Richmond. School had already started, and the administrators weren't sure whether to place Katherine in kindergarten or first grade, since she hadn't turned six yet. Finally, a decision was made based on two letters from her kindergarten teacher in Lynchburg, who was extremely impressed that Katherine could use scissors so well! Katherine's anguished practicing had paid off.

Or had it? She was miserable in first grade, no matter how well she could cut. For Katherine, the first grade was a strange mixture of boredom, terror, and sadness. She knew the other kids thought she was weird, perhaps even stupid. On Halloween she worried that she really was a Spook Baby. Here she was turning six, but none of her classmates wished her a happy birthday. She might as well have been a ghost.

By February, Katherine wanted only one thing: a friend. She had been waiting patiently for nearly a year, ever since arriving in the United States. She needed just one, somebody to play hopscotch with at recess, to walk home with after school. She had her eye on several girls and boys who seemed nice, but they were always busy with their buddies.

"Oh, Katherine, you'll make friends," her mother would say whenever Katherine looked glum. "Just wait and see. It takes time."

How she wished she were back in Huaian, where her friends would say happy birthday, where she wouldn't have to go to school. Her mother could teach her everything she needed to know. Her mother had already taught her to read, something Katherine's first-grade teacher didn't realize. Katherine was too shy to tell her; she found the woman frightening, like most of the teachers she'd met. And what was the point, anyway? She thought the books the teacher used to teach reading were *dumb*—baby books with few words and no story.

With no one to talk to and lessons she considered dull, Katherine became an expert daydreamer. One day, she imagined, she would come into class, sit down, and start reading aloud. Everyone would burst into wild applause, the teacher proudly announcing how brilliant she was and the kids begging her to read more.

And today, Katherine imagined, perhaps today, things might change for the better. Today was Valentine's Day. Her heart beat a little faster as she plunked herself down at her desk.

Maybe she'd get a card from some boy or girl who had been longing to be her friend but, like herself, was too timid to ask. Maybe she'd be invited over to someone's house. At the very least, she'd have some cards to open, some proof that she wasn't invisible.

She carefully tucked the valentines she was going to distribute inside her desk. She'd spent hours working on them, carefully choosing the right card for each classmate. Now she needed to be patient until the festivities started.

First were lessons in reading, math, and spelling. Katherine tried halfheartedly to pay attention, but she found herself thinking about all that had happened since she came to the United States. She squinted at the hands of the clock on the classroom wall, trying to make sure they were still moving. *Just barely,* she decided. Valentine's Day must be the slowest day of the year.

Finally, near the end of the day, the teacher announced that the fun could begin. At first, Katherine watched as the other students dropped their envelopes on each other's desks. Then she began to make her own deliveries, wondering what surprises might be waiting when she came back. She took her time, making sure to look cheerful, but carefully hiding her excitement.

A few minutes later, after handing out her last card, she returned to her desk.

It was bare.

She looked inside, as though searching for a pencil.

Nothing.

She opened her books, pretending to read them.

Nothing. Not one valentine.

Katherine sat very still, gripping the edge of her desk, trying to hold back her tears.

She managed to keep them inside until the bell rang and she finally got home. She threw open the door and hurried inside where Sonny and Lizzie were each showing their mother handfuls of valentines. Katherine took one look and ran to her room, slammed the door, and threw herself onto her bed.

America is the loneliest place in the world, she thought, sobbing.

None of the Womeldorfs ever forgot the day Katherine didn't get any valentines. The memory always saddened her mother, who, once Katherine became a writer, often asked, "Why don't you write a story about that day?"

"But Mother," Katherine would reply, "*all* of my stories are about the time I didn't get any valentines."

Chapter 5
Back to China

Once the movie began, though, I was swallowed up in its magic. The real world of war and homesickness and fear seemed to disappear. . . . I loved those songs, especially "Somewhere Over the Rainbow." I longed to go over the rainbow. It sounded more like heaven than the place we sang hymns about every day and twice on Sundays.

"Why I Never Ran Away from Home"
When I Was Your Age: Original Stories About Growing Up

Not long after that dreadful Valentine's Day of 1939, the Womeldorfs were allowed to return to China. But since Chinese Communists, Nationalists, and Japanese troops continued to fight, the country remained unsettled. Traveling back to Huaian was still unsafe for Mrs. Womeldorf and the children, so they went to Shanghai.

The danger didn't stop Mr. Womeldorf, however. He had been asked to take desperately needed medicine from Shanghai to a missionary hospital near Huaian. The delivery had to be secret; drugs were considered contraband, or illegal, because they were in such short supply. If the drugs were spotted by anyone—Chinese officials, Japanese invaders, or bandits—they would be stolen. To hide them, Mr. Womeldorf built a false bottom in his steamer trunk.

At one point during Mr. Womeldorf's mission, a Chinese inspector working for the Japanese occupiers opened the trunk and began to search its contents. Mr. Womeldorf felt sure the drugs would be discovered, but another inspector intervened, saying, "Don't you know this man would never do anything to hurt our people?" Mr. Womeldorf was allowed to continue his journey, and, finally, after weeks of nerve-wracking difficulties, he delivered the medicine.

Katherine knew nothing of his heroism until much later, when she was an adult. Sometimes, however, all the fears of her childhood overcame her. One night she had a vivid dream that she was part of a group of Christians being held captive aboard a ship on a stormy night. She and the others were ordered to lie down on crosses—they knew they would be killed. Suddenly a strange light appeared in the sky. Katherine recognized the light as Jesus and knew she was safe. The dream that had started out as a nightmare ended up being an enormous comfort, something she always remembered during frightening times.

After a brief stay in Shanghai, where the children attended the Shanghai American School, she and the rest of the family traveled north to a beach house in Qingdao, a resort on the Yellow Sea. For Katherine, the summer was a strange combination of magic and sheer terror.

During the mornings and afternoons she loved playing in the water with her family; in the evenings many of the missionary families got together to enjoy what was left of the day. Because Qingdao was quite far north, the sun didn't set until late, giving the days an endless, leisurely feel. One night Katherine heard someone say it was after nine o'clock. She had never stayed up so late; what's more, it was still light outside.

The adults relaxed and swapped stories while the children played. Their favorite game was to hide from a young missionary woman who pretended to be a witch and chased them. Katherine loved the squealing, scary excitement.

But there was real-life danger as well. Japanese soldiers practiced their maneuvers on the beach right outside the house where the Womeldorfs were staying. These were not attacks, simply practice sessions; however, the officers loudly boasted that they were getting ready to invade the United States, to storm onshore in San Francisco. Often they conducted exercises in the middle of the day, a time when Mrs. Womeldorf made it a rule to keep her children inside, out of harm's way.

One day, however, Katherine and Helen were still out when the drills began. Mrs. Womeldorf was inside with the other children; a Chinese woman was looking after the two middle girls, who stood at the edge of the yard, lost in their world of make-believe.

"ARARRR!"

A blood-curdling roar filled Katherine's ears. She looked up the beach. There, charging toward her, were hundreds of Japanese soldiers dressed only in loincloths, their guns and bayonets drawn.

Katherine screamed. She grabbed Helen, nearly yanking

her off her feet, and they ran toward the house. Heart pumping, Katherine ran as fast as she could, dragging her sister along. She was so scared she kept her eyes closed.

As they reached the door, the Chinese woman pulled them to safety. Once inside, Katherine and Helen fell into their mother's arms, and the door was slammed shut.

Katherine couldn't stop crying. The roar outside grew louder as the soldiers streamed by.

"Oh, Momma," she said, "the Japanese were going to kill us."

"I saw you," Mrs. Womeldorf kept saying. "I saw you but I couldn't get to you in time."

The soldiers weren't trying to hurt the girls; they probably didn't even see them. However, Katherine and Helen might have been trampled.

Once fall came, the Womeldorfs returned to Shanghai, where they found refuge within the walls of the Shanghai American School. Since many families there were British, Katherine began to speak with a British accent. She hadn't spoken Chinese for such a long time that she had forgotten how.

In contrast to their haven, the city outside the gates was terrifying, full of needy people. When Katherine and her friends traveled by ricksha to the movies, begging children crowded around the vehicle, their faces dirty, their clothes ragged, their skin covered with sores.

For the most part, though, Katherine and the other children at the school were shielded from the turmoil, caught up in their own world. They were thrilled by the movie version of *The Wizard of Oz*. Katherine loved everything except the scary parts—the tornado, the Wicked Witch, and those flying monkeys. She covered her eyes until Lizzie poked her, the signal that it was safe to watch.

After moving many times and being frightened by bombs, soldiers, and bandits, Katherine sometimes felt like Dorothy, swept away by a tornado, uncertain where she might land. She felt lucky to have her own Auntie Em and Uncle Henry—her kind funny parents, who always helped her find her way. But she couldn't help missing her father. She knew she was supposed to be happy that he was taking care of the poor people in Huaian, helping his Chinese friends run the church and school, but sometimes it was hard to understand why he wasn't with her.

After seeing the movie, Katherine and her friends played Oz for weeks. Whenever Katherine sang "Follow the Yellow Brick Road" or "Somewhere Over the Rainbow," she felt sure she looked and sounded just like Judy Garland. Katherine wanted the role of Dorothy, but Lizzie informed Katherine that she wasn't pretty enough and didn't sing well enough. Since Katherine was small, she could be a Munchkin. Another girl who had long blonde hair got to be Dorothy, while Lizzie was the Wicked Witch.

Katherine couldn't believe how mean her own sister was being. "Lizard," she muttered. "Lizard. Lizard. Lizard."

Lizzie was too busy to notice. Wrapped in their mother's purple cape, she leapt at the other actors, cackling away. As soon as she appeared, everyone ran and screamed, just as they'd done back at Qingdao when the young woman had pretended to be a witch.

Katherine managed to distinguish herself in school. She didn't particularly like second grade, but it wasn't as terrible as it had been in Richmond, and she unknowingly began her literary career. Her first published work appeared in the school newspaper, the *Shanghai American*:

Pat! Pat! Pat!
There is the cat.
Where is the rat?
Pat, pat, pat.

In the late summer of 1940, before Katherine was due to start third grade, her father was appointed administrator of a missionary hospital on a hill in Zhenjiang, a city where the Grand Canal meets the Yangtze River. Housing was in such short supply that the Womeldorfs lived in a vacant hospital room.

Because there was no formal school, Mrs. Womeldorf taught her children in the morning, and during the afternoon they were taught by another missionary mother who lived in a compound on another hill. To get to her home, the Womeldorfs had to walk through a village in the valley below. Along the way they were greeted by the distinctive smells of Chinese food, farms, and animals. They also heard Chinese women keening—mourning—at the gravesides of men killed in the war. Their woeful cries were haunting.

Japanese soldiers made their presence felt in Zhenjiang in a respectful yet ominous way. Occasionally they interrupted Mrs. Womeldorf's lessons, asking various questions. Katherine and the children were supposed to go on with their lessons in the next room, but it was impossible to concentrate.

In December the Womeldorfs were informed that once again they must evacuate China and return to the United

States. Even though Katherine had been miserable in Virginia, the change sounded good in comparison to the frightening conditions in China. Helen and Anne, however, were too young to remember America and wanted to know what it was like.

"You're going to love it," Katherine promised. "You can buy anything you want!"

She glanced at her mother, hoping to be praised for her enthusiasm. Instead, Mrs. Womeldorf looked sad, almost tearful. Suddenly Katherine realized that her mother didn't want to leave. Hard as it was to live in China, her mother and father were devoted to helping its people.

Katherine looked away, her face reddening. It didn't matter that America seemed as alluring as the Yellow Brick Road and those magnificent ruby slippers. Instead of feeling like Dorothy, she felt like the Wicked Witch.

Chapter 6
War

"I was always made to feel stupid at school, and whatever it was that I was good at was not valued, and all the things that were valued, I was not good at, such as handwriting. . . . Even now, whenever I walk into a school, I still have this feeling that people are going to find something wrong with me."
interview with Katherine Paterson (spring 1996)

If you want to be a writer, Katherine Paterson might tell you that being an unhappy child isn't necessarily a bad way to start.

Before the fourth grade, Katherine had experienced sizable doses of fear and loneliness, many of them the result of politics and war. But in the fourth grade, where she was supposedly safe on American soil, away from all the turmoil, Katherine had her worst moments yet. She remembers those days as a "time of almost unmitigated terror and humiliation."

In the end, however, she would triumph, and out of that year grew many seeds she would eventually plant in her writing.

Before the dark days, however, came third grade, which Katherine completed in Virginia. Her second voyage to America was much less traumatic than her first. In fact, she fared better than the rest of her family and most of the other people on the ship, who got seasick.

Not Katherine.

Instead of being sick, she was hungry—quite a switch from when the German steward had to order her to eat. One day Katherine felt so famished that she announced, "Momma, they didn't ring any bells for lunch!"

Everyone stared at her from their bunks, looking pale and miserable.

"Oh, Katherine," her mother groaned, "nobody but you is hungry. There is no lunch."

Eventually the ship docked in Vancouver, Canada. From there the Womeldorfs took a train to Chicago and then to Lynchburg to Aunt Anne and Uncle Ernest's home.

Things were off to a good start. Katherine was happy to see her relatives again, and the Womeldorfs soon found a tiny apartment of their own. Katherine also found what she'd wanted so badly during her last stay in the United States: a friend.

Her name was Nancy Spencer. Not only was she Katherine's age, she was her second cousin. Nancy's family, which included twelve children, had moved to Lynchburg during the Womeldorfs' last stay in China.

Katherine spent lots of time at the Spencers' house. Mr.

Spencer owned a construction company, and the children were allowed to play with some of his building supplies stored in the yard. Nancy, Katherine, and the others spent hours building cinder-block cities.

In third grade, for the first time Katherine had a teacher who she felt liked her. She was ecstatic when the teacher asked her to play the witch in the class performance of *Sleeping Beauty*. Despite her shyness, Katherine loved being onstage. There, instead of being a refugee from halfway across the world, Katherine could be anyone, anything.

Katherine tried to be even more sinister than Lizzie had been playing the Wicked Witch in Oz. She cackled and narrowed her eyes at the girl playing Sleeping Beauty. Not until the final round of applause did Katherine stop leering. As the audience cheered, she felt like a star.

Later, with Katherine's family surrounding her, her teacher nodded at Mrs. Womeldorf and said, "Well, your Katherine really raised the roof today."

Mrs. Womeldorf smiled back, but Katherine wrinkled her brow. She knew she was being praised, but she wasn't sure how. Words, she was beginning to realize, could often be puzzling.

They could also be treacherous, she would soon discover, especially when they were spoken by bullies.

Soon after her ninth birthday, in 1941, the Womeldorfs moved from Lynchburg to Winston-Salem, North Carolina, where her father had been appointed missionary pastor of a Presbyterian church. Katherine hated saying goodbye to the first school that had made her happy, and, most of all, to Nancy.

The minute Katherine laid eyes on her new school, the Calvin H. Wiley School, she felt herself shrink. It was enormous, towering on top of a hill. Once inside, she wished she were invisible. None of the kids wanted anything to do with her. They kept their distance from the "Mish Kid," the missionary kid who spoke with a strange British accent.

She sounded funny and looked funny, too. Katherine's family couldn't afford new clothes, so they depended on church donations, known as clothing from the "missionary barrel." Some outfits were passable but others were shabby, and either way, Katherine knew they were hand-me-downs. Occasionally another girl would tell her, with tones of disgust, that the very outfit Katherine was wearing used to belong to her.

Things got even worse in December. On Sunday, December 7, Katherine and her family had gathered in the home of a family named Taylor. Because the church hadn't been built yet, the congregation met there to worship. The telephone rang, and after Mr. Taylor hung up, he stood staring, his mouth agape.

"What is it?" Mr. Womeldorf asked.

"The Japanese," he said slowly. "They've attacked Pearl Harbor."

Until that day, the United States government had gone out of its way not to become involved in World War II. But after about 2,400 Americans were killed during the surprise attack on the United States naval base in Hawaii, with more wounded and missing, the United States could no longer remain neutral. The next day, President Franklin D. Roosevelt declared war on Japan, and on December 11, Germany and Italy declared war on the United States.

During this time Katherine could hardly eat or sleep. She

felt the world would end any minute. After living in China, she knew what happened whenever Japanese soldiers dropped their bombs. After they bombed an area, they would invade, and then nobody would be safe. Maybe the same soldiers who had charged her with their bayonets were getting ready to storm American beaches.

On Monday, the day after the invasion, Katherine noticed that her classmates kept staring at her, sometimes whispering. At recess several of them surrounded her.

"You're not American, are you?" one boy said.

"Of course I am," she said.

"But you came here on a boat," another girl insisted. "I know it's true. I saw your family's picture in the news-paper."

A photograph announcing their arrival from China had showed the entire family drinking tea from Chinese cups. Katherine nodded, pleased the item had been noticed.

"I told you she's a spy!" the girl shouted.

The boy came closer now, nearly spitting in her face. "Jap!" he sneered. "Go back where you came from, Jap!"

Don't these people know anything? Katherine wondered, closing her hands into fists. She had been living in China, not Japan, and the Chinese were America's friends. The kids ran, leaving Katherine tearful, yet furious.

As the United States sent troops to Europe and the Pacific, Katherine's private war continued at Calvin H. Wiley. Out of necessity she developed a defensive strategy.

She knew she couldn't change her background, make herself bigger, or afford new clothes. The one thing she could change was her accent, which she practiced every chance she got, mouthing the words of her classmates and teacher. After a few months she started sounding like a native North Carolinian, an accent she would keep forever.

But this wasn't enough.

Katherine was convinced that everyone—including her teacher, Mrs. Black—thought she was stupid. The subject that made her feel the most insecure was handwriting. Back in Shanghai, she and her classmates had printed, but here, everyone used cursive. With her mother's help, Katherine was struggling to learn. The handwriting style her mother knew, however, varied slightly from the method used in Winston-Salem. Among other things, the letter "r" was made differently. Try as she might, Katherine couldn't master this new method, and, as a result, many of her spelling words were counted wrong. To make problems worse, erasing wasn't allowed.

These handwriting skirmishes worsened when Mrs. Black—who Katherine was certain must be 100 years old—left school. Most adults didn't discuss pregnancy around children in those days, but rumor had it that Mrs. Black was going to have a baby, which Katherine found hard to believe. Mrs. Black's replacement, Mrs. Hackler, was even more horrified by Katherine's penmanship than Mrs. Black had been.

Katherine's most terrifying battles, however, weren't on paper, but on the playground. The problem started over school rules, of which there were many. One of the main ones was that children were not allowed to walk on the grass. Although some of the off-limit "grassy" areas didn't actually *have* grass; the theory was that grass could grow if the children stayed off.

At recess one day, a girl shouted at Katherine. Katherine

thought she looked like a giant, and by no means a friendly one. "Me?" Katherine answered.

"Yeah, you," the giant said. "What's your name?"

The giant sniggered at her reply, then said, "Well, Katherine Wormy-dorf, I'm going to have to report you."

"W-Why?" Katherine said. She couldn't think of any infraction she might have committed.

"FOR WALKING ON THE GRASS." The giant dropped each word like a bomb.

Katherine looked down at her feet. There was no grass, only the red clay that covers much of the ground in North Carolina. She looked behind her, where she had just walked. No grass there, either.

"I saw you," the giant said, "and I'm going to tell the principal. You're in *big* trouble."

Katherine watched the giant walk over to some other girls, then point in her direction. She felt tears in her eyes. How could she have known this was a "grassy area" when there wasn't any grass? *Will I be kicked out of school?* she wondered.

Katherine spent the next few days living in fear. Every time a teacher looked at her, every time her name was called, every time the classroom door opened, she was sure her time was up, that she would be marched down to the principal's office, perhaps talked about in front of the entire school.

During this ordeal she learned the giant's name: Pansy. *How funny,* Katherine thought, *that such a hulk of a girl—a seventh grader—is named after a flower.* But the irony didn't make her feel better. Pansy gave Katherine long hard looks, reminding her that she was a Calvin H. Wiley criminal.

Finally, Katherine could stand it no longer. In music

class, as the rest of the students sang, Katherine began to cry. At first she shed just a tear or two, but then the drops turned into a steady stream. This would be the day, she felt sure, that the principal would summon her to the office.

The music teacher escorted her into the hall, signaling to the rest of the class to keep singing. "What's wrong?" she asked.

The words came out in a rush as Katherine confessed her crime. When she finished, she looked down at her feet, wondering why they had gotten her in so much trouble.

"It's all right, Katherine," the teacher said. "Nobody's going to punish you."

The teacher had to reassure her several times before Katherine would believe her, but finally the truth sank in. She wasn't an outlaw. As she headed back to the music room, Katherine thought how great it felt to go back to being Katherine Womeldorf, Mish Kid.

Just as the teacher predicted, Pansy never reported her. But Pansy didn't leave her alone, either. Although Pansy never hit her, her looks and words reduced Katherine to jelly. Sometimes she slung her insults alone and sometimes she brought other girls—Pansy's gang—all of them giants like herself.

The Calvin H. Wiley School felt like a dungeon, and Katherine needed a way out.

Chapter 7
Eye of the Hurricane

"I was never considered stupid again. I had some difficult times in school after fourth grade, but not because I felt I was being regarded as stupid. I really thought I was stupid in the early years."

interview with Katherine Paterson (January 1996)

In *Jacob Have I Loved*, Louise Bradshaw and her family weather a hurricane on their Chesapeake Bay island. As the eye of the storm passes overhead, the wind suddenly dies down, bringing a short-lived calm.

For Katherine, being a fourth grader at the Calvin H. Wiley School was almost like battling a hurricane day after day. Luckily, she found one place as peaceful as a hurricane's eye.

The library.

Back in China, she could hardly have imagined that so many books existed. As Katherine explored them one by one, Pansy and her teachers seemed far away and much less terrifying.

Katherine read book after book, especially anything by Robert Lawson, Kate Seredy, or Rachel Field. She loved the blend of history and comedy in Lawson's *Ben and Me*, the story of Benjamin Franklin as told by his mouse Amos. She was transported to Hungary when reading Seredy's *The Good Master*, about two European cousins on a ranch, and its sequel, *The Singing Tree*, about what happened to the cousins during World War I. She was thrilled by the exciting events in Field's *Hitty, Her First Hundred Years*, in which a wooden doll tells the story of her life, including voyages on a whaling vessel, a shipwreck, and her travels in India and the United States.

Best of all was Frances Hodgson Burnett's *The Secret Garden*. How Katherine would have loved to have a secret garden all her own; she was reminded of the Garden of Eden. She felt homesick for such a place, even though she knew the secret garden wasn't real. Even though Katherine wasn't an orphan like Mary Lennox, the book's heroine, she understood how Mary felt—so lonely and continually shuttled around from place to place. The book filled Katherine with hope. If Mary and sickly Colin could find joy, so could she.

Katherine may have been stuck in Calvin H. Wiley, but with books she could go anywhere: to the garden with Mary and Colin, to Paris with Ben Franklin and Amos, to Hungary

with cousin Kate, to India with Hitty. She could feel anything, depending on her mood, from glee with Amos to
sorrow with Mary. Back in Richmond she had longed for
one friend; now she had many.

She loved not only the stories, but the books themselves.
Touching them. Smelling their newness. Putting them back
on the shelves. Katherine became a library aide and was
asked to read stories to the younger classes. These kids, at
least, looked up to her. They didn't think she was weird.

Nor did the librarian. In fact, as time went by, Katherine
was given more responsibilities—arranging cards in the
card catalog, inspecting the bright new books, and pasting
pockets in the back of the books. But as much as she loved
processing the new arrivals, mending the old books was
even better. She dipped her brush into the glue pot like an
artist dabbing for paint.

Sometimes while shelving books, she had time to day-
dream, imagining herself as a movie star, a powerful but
kind queen, a fearless leader fighting Nazis and the
Japanese, or a hero being honored by President Franklin
D. Roosevelt. She could fly planes, break secret codes, run
behind enemy lines—anything.

Katherine had a secret, too. She knew no one else in
school but her (besides her sisters and brother) had met a
true hero or been kissed by one as well. The hero she knew
was her parents' friend, a woman named Miss Maude
Henderson. Miss Maude had grown up in Lexington, Virginia (where Katherine's father had grown up), become a
missionary, and started a home for abandoned baby girls in
Shanghai, where Katherine had met her. When Japanese
soldiers knocked on the door of the home, demanding the
girls, Miss Maude refused to budge, saying the soldiers

would have to kill her first. They backed off, although in the end she and the girls were placed under house arrest. Whenever Katherine thought of Miss Maude's courage, she hoped that she, too, could be brave in any situation.

Katherine had never particularly liked hugs or pecks on the cheek, and unmarried missionary women gave out many. But Katherine understood that a kiss from Miss Maude was special. When Miss Maude was a little girl in Virginia, her father had been a close friend of General Robert E. Lee, commander of the Confederate Army during the Civil War. Lee used to let little Maude ride on his horse. One evening he stopped by to visit her parents, and before leaving, he gave Maude a peck on the cheek. Then the general went home to eat supper. Unexpectedly, he fell unconscious and died. Maude, by a stroke of fate, was the last person he had kissed. To Katherine, being kissed by Maude seemed like being touched by history. What's more, her hero was one of the few people in the world who shared her heritage: someone with roots in both China and the American South.

Another of Katherine's favorite books was *The Yearling*, about a lonely boy from the South named Jody. Katherine knew just how alone he felt. The novel was also special because her mother had gone on a trip and brought it back as a gift for her. It was one of the many "flashlight books" that Katherine read in secrecy under the covers. As long as she was reading, dreaming, or working in the library, Katherine was happy.

Katherine even had some luck at school. A boy named Eugene Hammett invited her to a party. Her classmates thought Eugene was even odder than she was. He was chubby and wore round, wire-rimmed glasses, a style considered unfashionable at the time. Even worse, in their eyes, was the fact that he wanted to become a ballet dancer.

Katherine went to Eugene's party and had a good time. Afterwards, at school, he was always nice to her. Before long he was her best friend. One day he asked her why, if she was born in China, she wasn't Chinese.

"If a cat's born in a garage," Katherine replied, "does that mean it's a car?"

Eugene grinned. Finally, she had found someone who understood her. Maybe one friend was all she truly needed. With Eugene at her side, she got through fourth grade.

Somehow, after that, amazing things began to happen. In fifth grade she brought home a report card with straight A's. Her fifth- and sixth-grade teachers liked her and frequently praised her. Other students started to be nice to her as well. Perhaps they saw her and Eugene having fun, perhaps they saw her reading and working happily in the library, or perhaps they just got used to her. Katherine continued to work in the library, and also loved studying and reciting poetry, especially *The Song of Hiawatha*. She wrote plays, which she and others performed at recess and, occasionally, in class. One featured a rebel spy during the Revolutionary War.

By seventh grade, everyone at Calvin H. Wiley had forgotten that Katherine Womeldorf was supposed to be weird, maybe even a traitor. Instead of mocking her as they had once done, they elected her president of the student body.

Katherine was delighted, of course, but she hadn't really changed. Even though she had more friends and more confidence, she was often struck by moments of self-doubt.

She never forgot how it feels to be lonely, scared, and disliked.

Years later, when she began to write children's books, those memories became a treasure chest of sorts, something she dipped into to fill her books with genuine feelings and characters. When writing *Flip-Flop Girl*, for instance, she knew just how Vinnie Matthews feels when her mother takes her to a new school in Brownsville, how she feels on the playground when nearly everyone ignores her. In *Jip: His Story* she understands how nervous Jip is when he goes to school for the first time, and how he can't wait to hear what happens next as the teacher reads *Oliver Twist* aloud. When Jiro carefully tries to glue the puppet head his father has made in *The Master Puppeteer*, Katherine remembered how meticulously she had worked while repairing books in the school library.

Had Katherine not had such a miserable year as a fourth grader in Winston-Salem, her books might not be so rich.

Chapter 8
Where to Now?

All the parents in my stories are seen from their children's point of view, and it has been my experience that children are very seldom fair in their judgment of their parents. I hope I've sent all my questioners home to take another, more objective look not only at my book, but at their own parents, most of whom, I dare say, are like the parents in Bridge to Terabithia, *doing the best they can under trying circumstances.*

"People I Have Known"
The Spying Heart

The Womeldorfs were still planning to return to China once the political situation and economy improved after World War II ended. Finally, in the summer of 1946, Mr. Womeldorf got word that they could return.

By now Katherine's brother was in the United States Navy and Liz was about to enter college; only Katherine, Helen, and Anne would accompany their parents. Katherine knew she would miss her friends in Winston-Salem, but was excited to go back to Asia. While arrangements were being finalized, they moved back to the missionary apartments in Richmond. Mr. Womeldorf gave up his job at the Winston-Salem church and worked for the missionary board.

The Womeldorfs were still waiting to go abroad when the school year began. Katherine, now a freshman, was upset that ninth graders in Richmond attended a junior high, because she felt like a high school student. What she liked, however, was the fact that all of the new students were assigned to the same homeroom. This made adjusting to her classmates relatively easy, because everyone was new and in need of friends.

Especially Anita Carter, a girl who was even shyer than Katherine. Everyone else was shy around Anita because she was famous. She belonged to the Carter Family singers, who had cut more than 250 country music records. The group originally included Anita's mother, Maybelle, and Anita's aunt and uncle, but it later grew to include Anita's sisters and cousins. Anita was the youngest of three girls, but she was the first to join their mother onstage.

Katherine often heard the Carters on the radio and once saw them perform; she thought they were absolutely wonderful. Onstage, Anita's shyness faded like snow on a sunny day. In the classroom, however, she seemed like she wanted to hide.

Katherine was asked to tutor Anita, whose singing career had caused her to miss a lot of school. During their sessions Anita was nice, but so bashful that they never became close. Katherine felt sorry for her and was astonished to see how difficult it was for such a well-known person to make friends.

Nonetheless, Katherine still dreamed of being a famous movie star, especially after seeing Elizabeth Taylor, who was her own age, star in *National Velvet*. For now, though, Katherine's only hint of fame came from a play she wrote, a musical set in Mexico. She chose the setting because she and her classmates had been studying the country's music. Katherine didn't get the lead; that role went to another freshman girl.

Later, when Katherine became well-known for writing children's books, she noticed that many people she met treated her differently from others. On book tours she felt that people acted awestruck in her presence, as though she weren't a real person. She complained to her family about this special treatment, and she recalled how she and her classmates had felt nervous about talking to Anita Carter or including her in their fun. Katherine's memories of Anita prompted her to write *Come Sing, Jimmy Jo*, about an Appalachian boy named James, a talented country singer and guitar player.

Months passed and the Womeldorfs were still in Richmond. They had taken care of all the necessary preparations, such as taking shots to protect them from diseases in Asia. Katherine couldn't imagine the reason for the delay.

Despite their lack of money or a house of their own, one thing the Womeldorfs could always count on was their religious faith. About this time, however, Katherine read *Wuthering Heights*, Emily Bronte's tragic love story. She was plunged into despair, convinced that God didn't exist. Why the book had such an effect on her Katherine never understood, but she knew that she felt miserable and off-kilter.

Her distress was so evident that the mother of a friend introduced her to the theological writings of C. S. Lewis. Katherine started by reading "The Case for Christianity," a talk Lewis had given. His arguments made sense and helped restore her faith. Still, her ideas about God were changing. As a child, she had heard many ministers (not her father) describe God as a wrathful, judgmental being. They preached about judgment day and damnation, not love and forgiveness. Over the years Katherine replaced that wrathful vision with that of a deity capable of unconditional love, who loves people as parents love children: always—even when they make mistakes.

One day Katherine was rummaging through her father's desk, searching for some paper. She came across a letter from the missionary board, and, even though it was addressed to Mr. Womeldorf, curiosity got the better of her. She read it. The letter said that costs were now too high for the mission board to send three children to school in China, especially one as old as Katherine, who would have to be sent to boarding school. The board could only afford to educate the two younger children. If the Womeldorfs wanted to return to China, they must leave Katherine behind.

Katherine was devastated. *She* was the problem. She knew her father wanted to go to China more than anything, and she was the one keeping him from his dream. She shoved the letter back in the desk and went to her room. She thought about other missionary families they knew. Several parents had gone overseas and left their children behind. Katherine knew what had to happen now.

As soon as Katherine saw her father, she told him about her discovery.

"Katherine," he told her. "You don't understand. There are many reasons we're not in China yet." He began to reel off a list of explanations, none of which sounded very convincing.

This, Katherine thought, was the closest her father had ever come to lying to her. "There's just one reason," she said. "Me. I saw the letter."

Mr. Womeldorf grew quiet. There was no way around the truth, and both of them knew it.

"Go," Katherine cried, tears welling in her eyes. "Go without me!"

"Oh, Katherine," Mr. Womeldorf said, hugging her tightly. "Sweet girl, we would *never* leave you behind."

Katherine knew he meant what he said. Seldom had she felt so loved.

Katherine in China at age two

Katherine (center) at age four with her mother and father, sisters Lizzie and baby Helen, and brother Sonny in Kuling, China, the year before Anne was born

Katherine (front row, left), Sonny, and Lizzie (back row) in 1937 with some of their neighbors in Huaian

Katherine at age 11

Katherine and a friend visiting a puppet maker in Tokushima, Japan, in 1960

Katherine at age 28 with Kuroda Tokue in front of the house where they lived

John and Katherine on their wedding day, July 14, 1962

John, Katherine, and Manch, their first dog, in the summer of 1963

The Paterson family in 1967 celebrating David's first birthday

John, Lin, Mary, and David at Christmas, 1971

Katherine, John, and their children celebrating Katherine's Newbery Award in 1981

Katherine in 1983 with Blossom, her 13-year-old springer spaniel

John and Katherine with their children and grandchildren at John's retirement in June 1995

Part II
Finding Her Voice

The Womeldorf family never got a chance to return to China. By the time Katherine graduated from high school, the Communist government there had banned westerners. When the restrictions were lifted years later, Mr. Womeldorf's health was frail, and he didn't have the heart to return. The Communists had killed his best friend, Mr. Lee.

Families weren't supposed to stay in the missionary apartments for much more than a year, so after spending her freshman and sophomore years in Richmond, Katherine and her family had to leave. While Mr. Womeldorf continued to work for the missionary board, a minister in Charles Town, West Virginia, promised them a place to live. Charles Town was a small town, a place where all the high school students had grown up together, where Katherine was once again an outsider.

But not for long. On the very first day of school, a popular girl named Barbara Hughes introduced herself. Barbara decided immediately that she wanted Katherine as her friend, prompting the other students to welcome her as well. Barbara's friendship saved Katherine from what could have been two lonely, dreadful years.

In addition to Barbara, the best thing about the new school was dramatics. Katherine played Marmee in *Little Women*, sang lead in a revue, and played an old wife in a play called *The Blue Teapot*. She and the rest of the cast won a district competition and went on to the state finals.

At home, the Womeldorfs had an important visitor: Miss Maude Henderson, who had been forced to leave China by the Communists. She was old now, but neither age nor political strife had dimmed her spirits. As she savored one of Mrs. Womeldorf's scrumptious desserts, she said, "I've only got one tooth left, but it's all right. The doctor says it's my sweet one." Katherine looked at the bright-eyed woman with love and awe.

These were not the happiest times for the Womeldorfs, however. Katherine's mother was ill for a while, which meant that Katherine had to look after her younger sisters whenever their father traveled, a responsibility she disliked.

When Katherine graduated from high school in 1950, she was ready for a change. Since she knew the odds of becoming a movie star were slim, she set her sights on becoming a missionary, wife, and mother. The thought of being a writer never occurred to her.

College was exactly what she needed. She won a scholarship and worked her way through King College, a small liberal arts school in Bristol, Tennessee. There, for the first time in her life, she understood what learning was all about. Unlike many of her previous teachers, the professors at King didn't mind if she asked questions, no matter what they were. In fact, they expected students to challenge and analyze ideas.

During her sophomore year, Katherine decided to major in English. Her professors introduced her to many extraordinary writers, including Gerard Manley Hopkins, John Donne, William Shakespeare, and Emily Dickinson. They also praised her essays, encouraging her to do more writing. Whether in class, in her dorm, or onstage during a dramatic or choral performance, Katherine felt as though she belonged.

Upon her graduation in 1954, Katherine had a plan. She intended to teach for a year to get some experience and then attend graduate school to become a missionary. She found a position as a sixth-grade teacher in Lovettsville, Virginia. Now that she was going to be a teacher herself, she wondered whether the students would like her.

Chapter 9
Bridge to Adulthood

Lark Creek Elementary was short on everything, especially athletic equipment, so all the balls went to the upper grades at recess time after lunch. Even if a fifth grader started out the period with a ball, it was sure to be in the hands of a sixth or seventh grader before the hour was half over.

Bridge to Terabithia

Katherine looked around the small bedroom she now called home. *What was she doing here?* she wondered. She was living in a boarding house in Lovettsville, but contrary to the town's name, she certainly didn't love it.

It was pretty, she had to admit. Lovettsville sat in the valley of the Blue Ridge Mountains, right on the Maryland border, just a few miles away from Charles Town. But at age twenty-one she felt like such a different person from the high school student she had been that there might as well have been an ocean in between. Even her parents had left Charles Town; Mr. Womeldorf had become the associate pastor at a church in Winchester, Virginia.

Katherine was surprised at how lonely she felt. Another young woman who taught third grade roomed in the same house, but while her colleague was nice enough, she and Katherine didn't have much in common. After spending four years at King College, Katherine was used to having close friends on hand, ready to talk at practically any hour of the day. The magical world she had found at King was gone.

Instead, each weekday morning 36 students waited for her in a basement classroom. Lovettsville was a poor community, which meant the school was run-down, without a library or lunchroom. As for the students, Katherine had found a list of their IQ scores, many of which were quite low. Katherine shoved the paper into her desk and promptly forgot about it. There was no denying, however, that they were a motley crew. They ranged in age from 10 to 16, because some had failed a grade several times.

After the first day, many of Katherine's anxieties disappeared. No, she didn't know much about being a teacher, and she didn't think she was likely to be a particularly good one. But she couldn't have asked for a nicer group of students. They listened to her as though she were sharing magic spells. They loved hearing about life in China, about anything really, since they had a hard time imagining life beyond their valley. They had never had a teacher who had graduated from college or who had seen much of the world.

At first the basement classroom had seemed dark and isolated. Soon, however, Katherine realized that there, away from the rest of the school, they had their own little kingdom. On rainy days, for instance, they shoved back the desks and held broad-jumping contests. They could do things their own way without bothering anyone else.

Katherine brought her own books to school, reading aloud *The Lion, the Witch, and the Wardrobe* by C. S. Lewis. She read everything from *Huckleberry Finn* to Shakespeare, especially *Macbeth*, which the class loved because of all the gore. Sometimes she read word for word; sometimes she explained difficult sections and went on to the next.

During class discussions of history, Katherine explained how dates in western history were divided according to their relation to the birth of Jesus Christ: into years B.C. (before Christ) and those after his birth, known as A.D., for the Latin *anno Domini*, "in the year of the Lord." The concept was difficult for the class to grasp, so Katherine spent hours going over it. By the end of the day one Friday she was sure everyone understood, and she left school pleased that they had conquered a considerable lesson.

The following Monday, she started off with a quick review. One of the smarter girls raised her hand and said, "There's something I don't understand yet, Miss Womeldorf."

"What's that?"

"Were the dinosaurs between B.C. and A.D.?"

Whenever Katherine had a low moment or felt lonely for her friends, she told herself, *Something wonderful is going to happen today.*

Sure enough, she found something wonderful. One day, upon returning to her room after a long day at school, she picked up *War and Peace*. She immediately lost herself in Tolstoy's world of Russian royalty. The classic was her only link to the intellectual stimulation she had thrived on in college. She could hardly bear to put down the book once she started reading. From start to finish, it was one of her favorite novels, something she looked forward to every day.

The year's highlight for the sixth graders was a field trip Katherine arranged to Washington, D.C. Although the capital was only two hours away, the children had never been there, and Katherine was determined to give them an adventure.

They had been studying medieval life, so she arranged for a schoolbus driver to take them to the catacombs in Washington and to the Washington Cathedral. If everyone behaved, she promised, they could visit the zoo. The children obliged. By the time they got to the zoo, they had only an hour left before they had to drive back to Lovettsville. Thirty-five kids (one had stayed home) ran off in different directions, with strict instructions to be back to the bus by ten minutes before two.

As she watched them disappear, Katherine suddenly panicked. *What if they don't come back?* she thought. *What if they get lost?* She spent the next 50 minutes fretting, walking from exhibit to exhibit, often hearing whoops and hollers from her students.

At ten minutes before two she was greeted by the best sight of all: a long line of worn-out, happy kids. She relaxed and began to count heads.

"—31, 32, 33, 34."

Katherine stopped and looked around. Thirty-four?

One short. She glanced down the line of faces, swiftly taking attendance. "Godfrey," she moaned, wringing her hands. Godfrey was something of a troublemaker, so if anyone was going to be late, he was a likely candidate.

"Where is he?" Katherine asked. "Has anyone seen Godfrey?"

Just as she was envisioning a series of possible disasters—Godfrey injured, Godfrey lost—he popped out from behind a tree and bounded into the line. Katherine was so relieved she couldn't be mad at his little joke. She directed the children onto the bus and sat down, ready to head back to Lovettsville.

Suddenly she realized that everyone was accounted for—except the bus driver! He was the *last* person she had expected to be late.

Later that night, back in her room in Lovettsville, Katherine couldn't stop smiling about how happy her students had been. Something wonderful *had* happened.

By springtime a few of the boys in her class had fallen in love with Katherine; one sent a letter stating his undying devotion. Katherine was fond of all her students and knew she would never forget them, but she realized that teaching wasn't in her blood. She looked forward to continuing her studies in the fall.

A few days before the end of the school year, the class and principal surprised her with a farewell party. Even her family had been invited, and her mother and sister Anne came. Katherine couldn't get over how resourceful the children had been with their plans and how they had arranged everything without revealing their secret.

On her last day Katherine cleaned out her desk, trying to decide which papers to save, which to toss. As she pulled out some papers buried deep within her desk, she came across the list of IQ scores she had seen at the beginning of the year. This time she studied the names and numbers closely. Her jaw dropped. *These scores are all wrong*, she thought. *They are much too low. My kids are much brighter than this paper says they are.*

Katherine was both delighted and saddened—delighted that she hadn't paid any attention to the scores, but sorry to think how damaging such labels could be.

About twenty years later, when Katherine began writing the story of Jesse Aarons and Leslie Burke in *Bridge to Terabithia*, she modeled their school after Lovettsville Elementary and its students. Jesse and Leslie's fifth-grade classroom was in the basement; Lark Creek Elementary had no lunchroom or library. When the novel was published, Katherine felt sad because her students might never know she had written a book with them in mind.

In 1990, while driving to her 40th high school reunion in Charles Town, Katherine passed the sign for Lovettsville. On impulse, she decided to pay a visit.

A beautiful new school had been built. The old building was now used as a recreation facility and her old classroom had been converted to a day-care center. The room was longer and narrower than she remembered; she had a hard time believing this room full of cribs and playpens had once been hers.

She wandered over to the office of the new school and after explaining that she had once taught there, got permission to visit the new library. As she entered, the librarian nodded. The woman gave a distracted half smile, but looked hot and tired. Katherine explained herself once more, and the librarian asked her what her name was.

"Back then I was Katherine Womeldorf, but now I'm Katherine Paterson."

"You're kidding!" the librarian said. She set down a stack of books and stared. "*The* Katherine Paterson?"

Katherine nodded, embarrassed.

"You've made my day!" the librarian said. In no time at all she summoned other faculty members. The staff had a barrage of questions and asked Katherine to autograph copies of her books for the school.

The sixth-grade teacher beamed and said, "Every year I tell my students that *Bridge to Terabithia* is set in Lovettsville, but they won't believe me. Now they finally will."

Chapter 10
The Music of the East

In the course of four years I was set fully free from my deep, childish hatred [of the Japanese]. I truly loved Japan, and one of the most heartwarming compliments I ever received came from a Japanese man I worked with who said to me one day that someone had told him that I had been born in China. Was that true? I assured him it was. "I knew it," he said. "I've always known there was something Oriental about you."

"Sounds in My Heart"
The Spying Heart

After earning a master's degree at the Presbyterian School of Christian Education in Richmond, Katherine's dream of becoming a missionary was about to become a reality. But first Katherine needed to know where she was going to do her work.

Her first choice was China, but westerners were forbidden. Still, Katherine longed to return to Asia. A close friend in graduate school named Ai, a female pastor from Tokyo, suggested Japan. No, Katherine said. Even now, years after being stormed on the beach by Japanese soldiers, hearing their bombs and seeing their destruction, the memories still sent a flash of fear through her. Although she knew her apprehension was unreasonable, she had no desire to live with people she had once considered enemies.

"Think about it," Ai urged. "Give us a chance."

After careful consideration, Katherine decided Ai was right. In the late summer of 1957, Katherine was part of a group of missionaries and students who boarded a freighter bound for Japan. She would be gone for four years, first spending two years at language school in the city of Kobe, then working as a missionary for another two years.

Before reaching Kobe, the boat docked in Yokohama, a port city close to Tokyo. Since there was time to go ashore, Katherine decided to look up Ai, who had already returned to her country. Katherine convinced a woman she had met onboard to accompany her.

With Ai's address in hand, Katherine and her new friend, Jane, hailed a taxi. The driver took them into Tokyo, but once there, he stopped at a corner, unable to take them farther. Katherine hadn't known that Japanese addresses at that time indicated only a particular block, not an exact house or apartment building. Luckily, a policeman who knew the neighborhood was able to direct them to the right house.

By this time, Katherine felt uneasy. She couldn't speak or understand Japanese, except for one sentence learned during an orientation session before she left. The linguist in charge had discovered that a Bible verse from the book of John seemed to contain many important sounds in a variety of languages; she taught her students how to say: *A woman went down to the well to draw water* in Japanese. This phrase wouldn't be much help to her now, but Katherine had come this far, so she knocked.

An elderly woman answered. She was surprised to see two American women, but she invited them inside. Katherine and Jane took off their shoes and followed her upstairs into her living quarters, where they were directed to sit down. The woman spoke no English, so they had no idea whether they were in the right place. The woman stared for a moment, then indicated she would get some tea. When she returned, Katherine spoke her one and only phrase: "A woman went down to the well to draw water."

The woman looked puzzled, but nodded, as if in agreement. She kept disappearing for long periods of time; whenever she reappeared, Katherine greeted her with the Bible verse. She must have thought her visitor was crazy!

Finally, Katherine noticed a photograph of a large group of people on the wall. She examined it closely, and, sure enough, Ai was one of the crowd. At least she knew she was in the right place. Katherine pointed to Ai, then pointed to herself, trying to show that they were friends. The woman nodded and smiled, more vigorously this time, then left the room once more.

She came back and motioned for Katherine and Jane to follow her, leading them next door, where she handed Katherine a telephone. Evidently she didn't have one and had been arranging to use her neighbor's. A familiar voice greeted her through the receiver.

"Katherine, is that really you?"

It was Ai, who couldn't believe Katherine had been able to find her house and her mother. Ai taught at a nearby private school and came home right away.

The day ended magically. Ai took Katherine and Jane to a restaurant and invited a group of her students to perform traditional Japanese dances. Katherine hadn't even gotten to Kobe, and already she felt immersed in the new culture. Her fears began to fade. For one thing, no one wore uniforms. Instead of the soldiers she had encountered as a child in China, here were men, women, and children who seemed extraordinarily peaceful. After the horrors of World War II, the Japanese were determined to avoid another war.

Once Katherine was back onboard the freighter, she lay in her bunk and thought, *One friend. That's all it takes to break down old prejudices.*

While learning Japanese in Kobe, Katherine rented a room in the home of a prominent Japanese woman, the wife of a lawyer who had died during the war. Although she had a large house, Mrs. Kimura took Katherine in because she needed the extra income.

Mrs. Kimura lived downstairs with her sister and a maid, a woman who had worked for her since the early days of her marriage. Katherine took over the upstairs, which consisted of several spacious rooms, enough for an entire family. She shared the bath and kitchen, cooking for herself, although Mrs. Kimura occasionally invited her to dinner.

Before long Katherine had fallen in love with Japan. Being a foreigner, however, could be agonizing. New customs, such as sleeping on mats on the floor, were difficult at first. She was taken to a traditional tea ceremony, an ancient ritual she found strange and awkward. But she got used to most Japanese ways, except for the custom of sitting on the floor on her knees, which always made her legs numb. During church services she sometimes had to sit this way for two hours, and when she was introduced as a visitor, she could barely stagger to her feet.

In many ways Katherine's confusing exchange with Ai's mother was a forerunner of frustrations she would feel for the next year or so. Little had Katherine anticipated that words, not people, would be her biggest problem. She studied Japanese diligently, but she wasn't fluent for many, many months. Whenever Japanese friends took her anywhere, she often didn't know where she was going or whom she would see. Once there, while everyone else laughed and talked, Katherine watched in silence.

Things got even worse as she began learning simple words and phrases. People treated her like a two-year-old, trying to guess what she was saying, putting words in her mouth, or correcting her pronunciation and grammar. It was as bad as being in first grade all over again, when she couldn't figure out what her teachers wanted.

Mrs. Kimura was a big help. Often, when Katherine used her telephone, her landlady apologized for listening and intruding, then suggested different phrases for Katherine to use. Mrs. Kimura was so patient and helpful that Katherine never minded her advice. She picked up many idioms and subtleties of Japanese that weren't part of her classroom training.

After Kobe, Katherine went to work on Shikoku, the smallest of Japan's four islands, where a group of pastors invited her to help with Christian education. She lived in the northernmost province of Tokushima, a rural area devoted to fishing. Its rice paddies and fruit groves were quite a change from cosmopolitan Kobe.

The home she lived in belonged to a family named the Kurodas. It wasn't nearly as nice as Mrs. Kimura's house, but Katherine was friendly with the couple, their two children, and the woman's parents, who lived with them. The husband, a merchant seaman, was gone much of the time.

Katherine soon learned that her new landlords were part of a militant Buddhist sect known, ironically, for fierce anti-Christian beliefs. One day Katherine asked Mrs. Kuroda whether it troubled her to have a Christian living in her house.

"Oh no," she quickly replied. "Religion and renting are two different things."

One friend, one tenant, or one landlord, Katherine thought. *That's all it takes.*

As it turned out, a more distressing part of the Kurodas' religion was their custom of chanting. They believed that chanting certain phrases over and over made wishes come true. They did so endlessly, sending a hum throughout the household that Katherine sometimes found nerve-wracking.

To escape, Katherine hopped onto her small motorcycle. She rode whenever she could, relishing the freedom to explore both the countryside and her thoughts. At various village churches she preached and taught Bible classes, in both English and Japanese, doing just the sort of work her father had done while riding a donkey in China. Now, more than ever, she understood why her parents had endured so many hardships over the years. The excitement of helping people and living in another country made up for the difficulties.

For a foreigner, Katherine's Japanese was now quite good. She continued to study with a private tutor, and she was able to compose sermons in Japanese. She spoke Japanese all the time, except when she was around other foreigners. She discovered that not only were her words different, but that her thoughts had changed, becoming somehow more Japanese.

She began to appreciate traditions she had initially found odd. An elderly scholar invited her to a tea ceremony and carefully explained the symbolism of each act. He explained, for instance, how the sound of the boiling water made him imagine the sound of wind in the pines and how the clinks heard during the mixing of the tea symbolized the distant sound of a woodcutter's ax. Later, when another friend asked her to tea to celebrate Katherine's safe return from a trip, Katherine understood the rite as an act of love. The age-old ceremony represents Zen Buddhist principles of harmony, respect, purity, and tranquillity, qualities Katherine could now appreciate from an Asian perspective.

The Katherine Womeldorf who rode past rice paddies and told fishermen and farmers about God and heaven felt like an entirely different person from Katherine Womeldorf, sixth-grade teacher and graduate student. Katherine liked this new, independent woman very much.

Katherine's four years in Japan passed quickly. She missed her family, but in the final year and a half, she felt strangely distant from them. They communicated by letter, not by telephone, so she didn't even get to hear their voices.

Much had happened while she was gone, including the marriage of her sister Helen.

Missing such a celebration was hard, but even harder was not being with everyone during bad times. Three relatives died within a few months of one other: her brother, Ray, had married and lost his wife; a favorite cousin lost her husband; and Uncle Ernest passed away. By the time Katherine heard the news of each, the funerals were over. She hadn't even known anything was wrong. She felt left out.

Although she knew she would be sad to leave Japan, it was time to go back to the States. Her Japanese friends were curious about what she would do once she was there. Several said, "I guess your parents have picked out somebody for you to marry." That's the way people became engaged in Japan at that time: parents picked out husbands and wives for their children, basing the decision on social and economic status, not love.

"No," Katherine explained. "Marriage doesn't work like that in our country."

One woman asked, "How old are you, anyway?"

"Twenty-eight."

"Oh, well," she responded. "Too old!"

Mrs. Kuroda remained hopeful, however, promising that if Katherine adopted their Buddhist ways and took up chanting, she would find a husband.

Once back in the United States, Katherine knew people would wonder why she was still single. At that time, women her age were expected to have families, not careers, and the majority married in their late teens or early twenties. She hoped to marry, *if* she found the right person. In Japan, Katherine had built her own life, and she had been happy.

Chapter 11
Three Pairs of Chopsticks

"My mother told her best friend something terrible had hap-pened: that I had gone to lunch with a minister from Buffalo. Her friend said, 'Why that's lovely. Maybe she'll get married and stay in this country instead of going back to Japan.' My mother replied, 'I've been to Japan, but I've never been to Buffalo.'"
          interview with Katherine Paterson (spring 1996)

Katherine lay in bed at her parents' home, trying to get used to sleeping on a mattress again. First she tried lying on her back, then her stomach. Neither position worked. Finally, she lay down on the floor. At last she could sleep.

Sleeping wasn't the only adjustment problem she was having. She was glad to see her family, but something important was missing. The Japanese part of herself felt silenced, aching to be heard. She longed to use the Japanese words she had learned to describe the places, faces, and voices she missed. With English she couldn't properly explain what she had seen and how she had changed.

Besides, she was nearly thirty, too old to be living with her parents. She spent the summer working for the missionary board, trying to tell people about Japan. Sometimes, though, she felt as though no one really heard what she was saying.

"These people," she told herself, "don't know the real me."

She couldn't wait to go back to Japan. But first, like all missionaries, she was required to spend a year in the United States.

It turned out to be a good year. The Presbyterian Board of Christian Education awarded Katherine a fellowship that allowed her to enroll in Union Theological Seminary in New York in the fall of 1961. For someone who spent much of her early childhood hating school, now Katherine couldn't seem to get enough.

She was worried, however, at the prospect of living in New York City. Specifically, she knew her classes would be on one side of the street and her dorm on the other, and crossing the street seemed risky. Although she had traveled the world on her own, she was hit with a classic case of her Hong Kong Syndrome.

She needn't have worried. Not only was the street quiet, with little traffic, there was a tunnel allowing students to cross with ease. Katherine shared a dorm apartment with four other women whom she enjoyed, and her classes were the most challenging she had taken yet, requiring all of her time and attention.

That is, until she met John Paterson, a handsome young minister from a church near Buffalo, New York. She met him during a two-week study program he was taking at Union, when he and a friend invited themselves to play bridge with Katherine's roommates. They were still getting ready when their guests arrived, so Katherine opened the door and chatted for a while. When her friends appeared, John asked, "Katherine, don't you want to learn how to play?"

Katherine watched for a few minutes, but she wasn't particularly interested in the card game. In any event, the doorbell rang. A professor wanted to speak with Katherine about a paper. She left, and when she returned, she said good night and went to bed.

The next morning John called to invite Katherine to lunch.

"Are you sure you mean me and not one of my roommates?" Katherine asked.

"Yes, you," John assured her.

Before returning to Buffalo, he invited her to come there for an Easter visit. Katherine could tell his intentions were serious—he wanted to date and perhaps marry her. She liked John immensely. Not only was he extremely good-looking, he was a lively mixture of seriousness and fun. But she felt nervous. "I don't know him," she complained to one of her deans. "Well, Katherine," the dean replied, "If you don't go see him, just how do you plan to get to know him?"

John proposed during the Easter visit. Katherine knew him better, though not well. But she liked what she saw; in fact, she loved what she saw. She accepted, and they were married on July 14, 1962.

Instead of returning to Japan, as she had planned, Katherine joined John at his parish. "You always end up with something different from what you expect," she often says. She missed Japan and her friends there, but she felt confident in her decision. Just as her father didn't want to leave Katherine behind to return to China, Katherine knew she couldn't leave John.

Nonetheless, that first year was difficult, because suddenly Katherine had no friends other than John, no studies, and no work. Things improved the next year when they moved to Princeton, New Jersey, where John enrolled in the seminary at Princeton University. Katherine applied for a job as a seventh-grade English and eleventh- and twelfth-grade sacred studies teacher in a private school, the Pennington School for Boys. The students, however, were troublemakers, nothing like the children she had taught in Lovettsville. These boys were so disobedient that the previous teacher had resigned in disgust.

"Do you think you can handle them?" the headmaster asked Katherine.

"I'll try," she said, not sure herself.

"It's not *try!*" the headmaster bellowed. "It's sink or swim!"

Katherine armed herself with a secret weapon, something she called "The Look." Back in college someone had once advised her, "When you're in front of the class and you feel a sort of rumble, you know something's going to happen if you're not careful. Just stand in front of your students and don't say a thing. Stare at them for all you're worth, and think to yourself as hard as you can: if you don't sit down and be quiet, I'm going to beat the living daylights out of you. Never say a word because that would ruin it. Just think as hard as you can." Katherine had never had to use "The Look" in Lovettsville, but she used it frequently at Pennington.

Some of the other teachers worried about her at first. For several weeks the drama teacher said she expected to see Katherine run out of the classroom in frustration. When nothing happened, she asked one of the boys for his opinion of the new teacher. "Oh, she's tough," he replied. "If anybody glances sideways, she gives you this look!"

Her students might have been scared of her, but they weren't particularly interested in sacred studies. One November day Katherine was describing the last days of the Kingdom of Israel, when kings were being assassinated one after another.

"The Bible is such a dumb book," one of the boys said. "All these people getting killed—that would never happen today."

"He's right," another said. "I don't see why we have to study this stuff. What's the point?"

Before Katherine could reply, the history teacher burst into the classroom. "President Kennedy has been shot," he shouted.

Everyone stared in disbelief.

The day after Kennedy's assassination, Katherine received some important news. This news, however, was cause for celebration—her doctor confirmed that she was pregnant. She continued to teach, and two weeks after school ended, she gave birth to a son, John Paterson, Jr.

Katherine and John were ecstatic. From the start they had planned to have two children and adopt two more, because they knew many children were in need of homes.

They had applied to an adoption agency soon after they were married. PoLin arrived from Hong Kong six months after John Jr. was born. Her name is Chinese for "precious life." Katherine and John decided to call her Lin.

Lin was two years old, tiny and scared. The one thing she loved to do was eat. Evidently she'd been malnourished at the orphanage. She wouldn't sleep. Whenever Katherine or John tried to put her in her crib, she would scream.

After several exhausting days, a Chinese psychiatrist who belonged to the Paterson's church agreed to visit to see if he could help. Katherine and Lin were in the kitchen when the doctor and his wife arrived. The psychiatrist's wife appeared in the doorway and called softly to Lin in Chinese. She quickly ran to Katherine's side.

"She's going to be all right," the woman told Katherine. "She knows you're her mother."

Katherine picked Lin up to comfort her. Meanwhile, the psychiatrist looked at Lin's crib and advised John to lower the sides because Lin probably wasn't used to such a high bed. This would also give her easy access to her high chair, since food seemed to be one of her few comforts. They put pillows beside the crib in case she fell out.

Lin was still in Katherine's arms, nearly asleep at this point. As Katherine eased her into the crib, Lin jerked awake, as usual, but this time she looked around and relaxed. After a moment, she fell asleep. From that point on, she settled into her new life and family.

In 1966, John became pastor of a Presbyterian church in Takoma Park, Maryland, a suburb of Washington, D.C.

A few weeks later David Paterson was born. He looked so much like his older brother that Lin soon announced that she wanted a sister who looked like her.

Two years later five-month-old Mary arrived, born in Arizona at the White River Reservation of the White Mountain Apache. At the airport, when Lin held her for the first time, she said, "She's got the same color hair and the same color eyes and the same color ears as me!"

The family was complete. Katherine had finally found her missing chopstick, and now she and John had two pairs of their own.

Chapter 12
Fifteen Minutes a Day

When she was enrolling the children in new schools after the family moved . . . the clerk filling out the necessary forms asked Katherine her occupation. "I'm a writer," Katherine explained. "What do you write?" the clerk inquired doubtfully. "Children's books." . . . at that point the clerk smiled very sweetly and said, "Why don't we just put down housewife?"

profile by Gene Inyart Namovicz
The Horn Book Magazine, August 1981

Katherine became a children's writer by accident. After being a missionary and a graduate student, motherhood was a dramatic change. She loved her new role, but it was so demanding that she sometimes lost sight of herself. She decided she needed a new goal, something, as she put it, that wouldn't be eaten, dirtied, or torn apart by the end of each day.

But what? She had never considered anything except missionary work. In graduate school, one of Katherine's professors, Sara Little, had read one of Katherine's term papers and asked Katherine if she had ever considered becoming a writer.

No, Katherine had replied. She was studying some of the best writers in the English language, people like Tolstoy and Shakespeare. How could she ever hope to compete? She didn't want to risk being mediocre.

Maybe that's what God was calling her to be, Professor Little had responded. She added that unless Katherine was willing to risk mediocrity, she would never achieve anything at all.

That was the end of that conversation, until about the time John Jr. was born. Sara Little suggested that the Presbyterian Board of Christian Education hire Katherine to write a book for fifth and sixth graders to use in church school. Katherine was flattered and agreed. The project was much more difficult than she had imagined it would be. She was writing for a committee of people, each with different, sometimes opposing, opinions.

At long last the result was a book called *Who Am I?* It discusses many of the same questions Katherine would later pose in her fiction: Where is God? Where do I belong? What is my purpose? It's written in Katherine's trademark easy-to-read style and contains interesting, amusing stories mixed with thought-provoking discussions of religion. Katherine didn't know it yet, but she was on her way to becoming a children's writer.

Writing was one job Katherine could do as a mother. She wrote while the children napped or slept, grabbing at least fifteen-minute work periods each day, sometimes more, especially as the children got older.

About a year after moving to Takoma Park, a woman in

the church invited Katherine to accompany her to an adult education class in creative writing. Katherine tried her hand at articles, stories, and poems for adults, concluding that she enjoyed writing fiction more than nonfiction. She began sending her work to various magazines with hopes of being published.

She wasn't.

She kept at it for seven years—writing, mailing, and being rejected. In all that time she had one story published, in a small Catholic magazine that soon folded. The story was for adults, based on someone she had known in elementary school who would lie down in front of cars to see if they would stop. She also sold a poem, but this time the magazine went out of business *before* her work appeared.

One of the courses Katherine and her friend took was writing for children. Katherine decided that since her adult stories weren't selling, she might as well try writing a children's book, working on a chapter each week. She settled on a historical novel about Japan, since the project would give her an excuse to do interesting research and help her feel as though she were Japanese again.

Although having young children left her little time to write, her family often helped to inspire her. While Katherine was trying to decide on the plot of her book, Lin, then five, began having problems. Sometimes the little girl seemed to shut down. She wouldn't speak, wouldn't look at anyone, wouldn't cry; she just sat and stared. Katherine tried talking and holding her, but nothing worked. She had these spells frequently, and they terrified her parents.

One evening Lin sat on a kitchen stool and began to stare as her mother cooked. Katherine asked Lin a few questions, with no response. Finally, in utter frustration, she shouted, "Lin, if you don't tell me what's wrong, how in the world am I going to know what the problem is?"

This time Lin answered, saying, "Why did that woman give me away?"

Lin was trying to make sense of her birth and adoption. Katherine and John had never hidden the truth from Lin: her mother had abandoned her; a policeman had found her and taken her to an orphanage.

Katherine took Lin in her arms. "I think she put you where she knew you would be found and taken care of. She did it because she loved you."

"Is she alive?"

"I don't know."

"Is she all right?"

"I don't know, but I hope so."

After their discussion, Katherine began to wonder what it would be like to not know whether a parent was okay or even alive. This, then, would be the plot of her book: a boy, whom she called Muna, goes in search of his father, a *samurai*, a noble warrior, during the twelfth century. While the children were in school, Katherine spent hours in the library learning about daily life in twelfth-century Japan. Then she came home and wrote, rewrote, and polished. When she felt she was finished, she decided to call her book *The Sign of the Chrysanthemum*.

Her classmates were critical. So were seven publishers who rejected it. In 1970 she sent her manuscript to an eighth, Crowell. An editor there had just returned from a trip to Japan and liked Katherine's story. The editor said the company would publish Katherine's book, although she might have to wait several years. Katherine agreed, and the book came out in 1973.

Katherine realized that while the writing class had helped her discipline herself to write regularly, her classmates' suggestions and criticisms had not been helpful. From that point on, she became what she calls a "secretive writer." She doesn't share a manuscript with anyone or even discuss its plot until she's completed a first draft. The first person she shows it to is John, her first editor, who always has helpful and insightful comments. John has always been always her biggest supporter, telling her she had the makings of a successful writer, that she could find her way around any obstacle. The children were also important cheerleaders. Once Katherine began working on revisions, she read them each manuscript out loud or let them read it on their own.

Katherine also used twelfth-century Japan as the setting of her next book, *Of Nightingales That Weep*. A friend asked her to write a book with a female heroine, a strong person who overcomes many difficulties, because the friend felt her daughter needed such a story. Katherine tried, thinking such a character would also be a useful role model for Lin and Mary. During the course of the writing, however, Takiko, the heroine Katherine invented, took on her own personality. She is indeed strong, but also vain and selfish—in other words, a well-rounded character with both good points and bad.

Katherine knew that she must be true to her characters, their stories, and the social realities of their times—in this case, twelfth-century Japan. In that era it was nearly impossible for Takiko to be a feminist according to modern standards. *Of Nightingales That Weep* was published in 1974. It wasn't the story that Katherine had set out to write, but it was a book of which Katherine could be proud.

By the time Katherine started writing her third novel, her children were avid readers, so she asked them what kind of book they would like.

A mystery, they agreed.

Katherine was reluctant. "I like mysteries," she told them. "You know I do. But it takes a certain kind of brain to write them, and I don't have that kind of brain. I haven't been able to beat Lin at chess since she was six."

The children said that although she might have trouble writing a mystery, they believed such a book was likely to sell more copies than her first two had.

"Well," she said. "I'll at least try to write an adventure, one with plenty of suspense."

When reading the newspaper a few days later, Katherine saw a photograph of a Japanese warrior puppet, part of Bunraku, a classical form of Japanese puppet theater. While in language school in Kobe, Katherine had traveled to nearby Osaka to see Bunraku performances. She remembered how sinister and nearly alive the puppets had seemed. A puppet theater, she decided, was the perfect setting for a mystery.

Further inspiration appeared one night in a dream. While half awake, half asleep, she envisioned a boy on the second floor of an old Japanese warehouse. He was grabbing, looking for something—Katherine didn't know what. Then she heard ominous footsteps, and at the top of the staircase a white warrior puppet appeared, along with the black-hooded form of a puppeteer. That was all she saw, but she knew she had to write a story to explain such a vivid, compelling scene. Who was this boy? What was he searching for?

John suggested researching Bunraku in Osaka, Japan.

Katherine pointed out that they couldn't afford such a trip. Call your publisher, John said, and explain that you need your advance doubled. Katherine summoned her courage and got what she asked for. The trip was set for the fall of 1973.

Ever since Lin had started wondering about her adoption, she had asked to visit the orphanage that had once been her home. (Mary, in contrast, had no interest in tracking down her roots.) Katherine took Lin along and planned a stop in Hong Kong.

Lin couldn't remember being at the orphanage. The grounds were beautiful, overlooking the China Sea, but the buildings were stark and understaffed. Katherine and Lin were particularly interested in the girls who were Lin's age. The ten-year-olds slept on wooden bunk beds, ten to a room. Lin contrasted the scene to her comfortable room in Maryland, full of toys. Most of these children had never seen an American girl; they wanted to touch Lin and feel her clothes. Lin was shy, but she let them. She had hoped to learn more about her birth family, but there were no clues other than what she already knew.

When they visited the area for babies, the director pointed to a sad-looking two-year-old girl in the back of the room. "I bet she looks something like you looked, Lin," she said, "when you left for America." Lin stared at the toddler.

Later, when she and Katherine were alone, Lin said, "I guess that girl couldn't be my twin, could she, Momma?"

"No Lin," Katherine said. "That wouldn't be possible." Katherine imagined how her daughter must feel, as though some part of herself was missing. Nonetheless, Lin returned home knowing she was a Paterson through and through, now more than ever.

Katherine came back with notebooks of information for her book. She and Lin had attended Bunraku performances and had talked with puppeteers and other experts. They had learned about daily life in late eighteenth-century Osaka—where the novel would be set—and how it had been torn by civil disorder, plague, and famine.

With so much material, Katherine was sure she could write the novel quickly, but for some reason, she got stuck. She created a protagonist, Jiro, who is the son of a puppet maker and works as an apprentice in Osaka. She liked the contrast between the strict order of the puppet theater and the chaos on the streets. But try as she might to piece together the many details she had learned, the story felt dull and fragmented. Every day when she sat down at her typewriter, she thought, *I can't do this.* She kept at it, though, until she completed a first draft. But she wasn't pleased and nearly threw it away.

Then calamity struck. In the spring of 1974 Katherine learned she had cancer and needed an operation to remove a tumor. For several months after the surgery, she didn't have the energy to look at her manuscript. Even though doctors described her prognosis as hopeful, she was terrified she might die, leaving behind John and the children. Katherine had wanted suspense in her mystery, but not in her life.

Chapter 13
Matters of Life and Death

"I have been afraid of death since I was a child—lying stiffly in the dark, my arms glued to my sides, afraid that sleep would seduce me into a land of no awakening or of wakening into judgment. As I grew up, the fear went underground but never really went away."

Newbery Award acceptance speech
for *Bridge to Terabithia*, June 1978

While Katherine was ill, another family drama had been taking shape. During the first grade, David had gone to a small school near home, but the building was so old that the county decided to close it. In second grade he was sent across town to a school that was bigger, newer, and better.

David, however, was miserable. He loved to draw, but his new classmates called his pictures "stupid." Each day he announced he was never going back.

One day he came home and told Katherine, "Me and Lisa Hill are making a diorama about *Little House in the Big Woods*." With his new friend Lisa, school suddenly became exciting. She not only liked his pictures, she made him feel as though they could talk about anything. They played on the same T-ball team. After school David often went to her house, where they explored the nearby woods Sometimes she called David on the phone, and John Jr. would say, "It's your *girl* friend, David."

But they weren't boyfriend and girlfriend, simply best friends. Katherine knew that few people, especially second graders, are lucky enough to have such a special relationship.

Once summer came and school ended, David and Lisa saw less of each other. The Patersons spent July on Lake George, New York, where they rented a barn that had been converted to a cabin. Katherine was feeling strong enough to work on her novel, but she still worried that the cancer might return.

One evening a thunderstorm left them without electricity. The children were nervous and bored, so Katherine began to read aloud from her manuscript by candlelight. As she read, she noticed problems in the story, but she started feeling hopeful about it.

The next day she discovered John Jr. rummaging through her desk, searching for the manuscript. He couldn't wait to see what would happen next. Now Katherine knew she had a good story. Perhaps the worst of her troubles were over.

Not long after the Patersons returned home from Lake George, the phone rang. Katherine was reading a book called *A Grief Observed*, written by C. S. Lewis about the death of his wife. Katherine was still struggling with the possibility that she might die.

Katherine picked up the phone and heard some devastating news. Lisa Hill was dead. She had been struck by lightning while vacationing at Bethany Beach, Delaware, and had died instantly.

How could something that horrible happen? Katherine couldn't bear to tell David; she found John first. Then she forced herself to tell David. He didn't want to believe her.

Slowly the truth sank in.

John presided over Lisa's memorial service. David was upset because Lisa's Brownie troop sat in the front rows of the church, while he, her best friend, sat behind them. He consoled himself by drawing a picture for Lisa's mother, a funny one to help her feel better.

Once school began, David missed Lisa more than ever. His classmates teased him about being in love with a dead girl. Ignoring their taunts, he pretended Lisa was still there. He remembered how the two of them had sat in a corner in music class and loudly sang "Free to be You and Me." But when David listened for Lisa's voice, he heard nothing. He realized he was all alone.

"I know why Lisa died," he finally told his mother. "Because God hates me. He's going to kill Mary next."

He was certain God was going to punish him by killing everyone he loved. When his third-grade teacher, whom he adored, was hospitalized, he ran away from school, convinced he was responsible for her health problems. The principal found him sitting in a tree and tried to persuade him he was not to blame. The entire school staff was patient and helpful. Instead of criticizing him for not doing his schoolwork, they talked with him and sent him on special errands.

One of the things that most helped David heal was pottery lessons made possible by a gift of money from Lisa's grandmother. Lisa's mother also invited David and some of her daughter's other friends to plant some tulip bulbs that she and Lisa had planned to plant. Lisa would never be forgotten, and the pottery lessons and the tulips were representative of the creativity and growth inspired by her powerful spirit.

Difficult as it was, that fall Katherine returned to work on her mystery. Since she had to do something, she revised like mad. Now that she knew she could salvage the story, she felt a sense of purpose and direction. Katherine had included the warehouse scene suggested by her dream, but her editor, Virginia Buckley, didn't like it. Katherine couldn't bear to abandon the terrifying episode, and instead, reworked it. Her hard work paid off, because children tell her the warehouse scene is one of their favorites.

The Master Puppeteer was published in 1976. It won both a National Book Award for Children's Literature and a special award from the Mystery Writers of America. Katherine had written a mystery after all.

The January after Lisa died, Katherine attended a meeting of children's writers and publishers in Washington, D.C. At lunch someone asked how her children were.

Suddenly words tumbled out of Katherine's mouth as she spoke of Lisa's death and David's grief.

Everyone at the table was spellbound. When she finished, an editor suggested she turn the story into a book. The editor added, however, that the child shouldn't die by lightning because editors wouldn't believe such a tragedy was plausible.

Katherine had been nervous about writing a mystery, but she felt she couldn't write this story under *any* circumstances. How could she write about something she couldn't even bear to think about?

But she began. Perhaps she was so haunted by the events that she had no choice. At first nothing happened. She simply stared at a blank page of notebook paper. After several days she managed to scribble a few words. She wrote three pages, which began: "I am not sure I can tell this story. The pain is too fresh for it to fall into rational paragraphs, but I want to try. For David, for Lisa, for Lisa's mother, and for me."

Three pages became thirty-two, and she moved from notebook to typewriter, writing about characters she called Jesse Aarons and Leslie Burke. Her memories of Lovettsville provided the details she needed to describe Lark Creek Elementary. She invented the kingdom of Terabithia because she had invented imaginary worlds as a child. At first she thought she made up the name, but she later realized that C. S. Lewis mentions an island called Terebinthia in *The Voyage of the Dawn Treader*. She must have borrowed the name unconsciously. Lewis, for that matter, got it from the terebinth tree, mentioned in the Bible.

Katherine told no one about the book, not John, not David. But she knew that John Jr. was sneaking peeks, continuing the practice he'd started at Lake George. One night, however, he ran into the kitchen and shouted, "That boy started out to be me and now he's turning into David!"

No, she explained. She had been inspired by Lisa's death, but she was writing fiction, which meant she was creating characters, not describing people she knew. As a result, Jesse wasn't John, nor was Jesse David. Jesse was Jesse, her own invention. If anything, he was more like herself than anyone else—she drew on her own thoughts and emotions as she wrote.

Katherine kept writing. One day, however, she stopped, frozen. It was time for Leslie to die, and Katherine couldn't bear to make it happen. For days she stalled, doing anything else she could think of: housework, letter writing, arranging bookshelves, anything to avoid facing the terrible scene.

She was successful until a close friend asked about her work. Katherine revealed what she was writing about, saying, "I can't face going through Lisa's death again."

Her friend looked thoughtful, then said, "Katherine, I don't think it's Lisa's death you can't face. I think it's your own."

Katherine realized her friend was right. She was heartbroken over Lisa, but she was still terrified that she, too, might die.

What could she do? She couldn't bring Lisa back, and only time would tell whether her cancer would return. The only thing to do was write. She went to her study and closed the door. By the end of the day she had written the dreaded chapter. Several weeks later, she completed a draft of the book. She felt more work was needed, but she wanted Virginia Buckley's opinion.

One last step remained. She read the manuscript to David to gauge his reaction. She knew that even though Jesse wasn't David, everyone would assume he was. Katherine felt he had a right to say whether the story should be published. After listening carefully, he gave her the go-ahead, making one request—that the book be dedicated to Lisa Hill. She agreed and mailed off the manuscript.

Then came the hard part: waiting. *The book is terrible,* Katherine decided. *Virginia must hate it. She's probably going to tell me I should find another career.*

Virginia liked it, of course. She told Katherine she laughed through the first two-thirds of the book and cried through the rest. She offered helpful suggestions, saying Leslie needed to grow and change during the course of the novel. Suddenly Katherine remembered how Pansy had tortured her at Calvin H. Wiley, and she created a similar character named Janice Avery, along with Janice's cohorts, Wilma Dean and Bobby Sue Henshaw—all perfect foils for Jesse and Leslie. Now that she knew the story was going to work, Katherine felt joyful as she revised.

She was told more details were needed to convince readers that Jesse was truly an artist, that he not only drew but thought like an artist. Katherine searched several sources for inspiration, such as letters written by the French painter Vincent Van Gogh, but nothing helped.

Finally she turned to David. "Why don't you ever draw pictures from nature?" she asked him, without explaining her mission.

"I can't get the poetry of the trees."

The line was exactly the sort she needed; she put the words right in Jesse Aarons' mouth. This is the only time she ever consciously used a real-life line of dialogue in one of her books.

The final touch was the dedication. Katerhine wanted to be sure that everyone knew her work of fiction had been inspired by David's grief for Lisa Hill. Katherine said:

> I wrote this book
> for my son
> David Lord Paterson,
> but after he read it
> he asked me to put Lisa's name
> on this page as well,
> and so I do.
> For
> David Paterson and Lisa Hill,
> *banzai.*

The last word was the only one she knew that adequately summed up her feelings, a Japanese word that combines the meaning of the English word "hooray" with the ancient Japanese salute to royalty, "Live forever!" She thought Leslie Burke would have liked such a victorious roar.

Once *Bridge to Terabithia* was published, Katherine and David took a copy to Lisa's mother. She liked it. Lisa's older sister had said one of the hardest things about Lisa's death was her worry that nobody would ever know about her. Now children around the world would.

Bridge to Terabithia won the Newbery Medal in 1978. Katherine accepted the award in front of a huge audience of librarians, editors, and writers in Chicago, as well as her family. In her speech she talked about her cancer, her fear of death, Lisa's death, and her struggles to write the book, concluding:

> *It is a strange and wonderful thing to me that other people who do not even know me love Jesse Aarons and Leslie Burke. I have given away my own fear and pain and faltering faith and have been repaid a hundredfold in loving compassion from readers like you: As the prophet Hosea says, the Valley of Trouble has been turned into the Gate of Hope.*

When she finished her speech and returned to her seat, Katherine noticed that the president of her publishing company was crying.

In her nervousness, her first thought was that she had said something wrong and had somehow embarrassed the company.

No, she was told. *Everybody* was crying.

Chapter 14
Vorin's Gift

Nobody wants to tangle with the great Galadriel Hopkins. I am too clever and too hard to manage. Gruesome Gilly, they call me. She leaned back comfortably. Here I come, Maime baby, ready or not.

The Great Gilly Hopkins

"Mom, can we adopt one of those kids?"

Katherine wasn't sure which of the children was asking this time. All four wanted another brother or sister, maybe several, even though Katherine and John firmly agreed that their own four children, now ranging in age from seven to ten, were all they could handle.

"Those kids" in question appeared on the evening news night after night, young Cambodian refugees being airlifted out of their homeland. In April 1975, Cambodian Communists known as the Khmer Rouge had taken over Cambodia, instituting policies that would eventually lead to the deaths of one million people. Cambodian parents were making frantic attempts to put their children on buses or take them to airports—anything to get them out of the country to safety, even though they might never see them again.

Katherine's heart ached as she watched the television footage. When she and John got a call asking them to be foster parents to two Cambodian brothers for two weeks, until a more permanent home could be found, they quickly agreed. Since the children's parents were still alive, they couldn't be adopted.

Two weeks? Katherine thought. *We can manage anything for two weeks.* She and John put bunk beds in the boys' bedroom to make space for the visitors.

The Patersons were told little about the background of the brothers, named Vorin and Pitou, only that all of the refugee children had been put on a plane in Cambodia with no passports or papers, just name tags around their necks. The plane flew to Thailand, but American relief workers didn't know what to do with them, so they were flown to San Diego, California.

As it turned out, some of the children were Cambodian, some Vietnamese. Social workers in California sent the Cambodians to Washington, D.C., and the Vietnamese to Chicago, where foster homes were being arranged.

Once Vorin and Pitou arrived in Washington, they told social workers some startling news. They had another brother, but he had disappeared in the California airport. Amidst all the confusion, the eight-year-old had wandered off from his brothers and ended up on the Chicago-bound plane with the Vietnamese children. Because the boys did not speak English, they couldn't explain the problem right away.

Now, however, social workers were trying to locate their missing brother and have him flown to Washington. The Patersons would be kept informed of their progress. They were also given the phone number of a Cambodian man, someone the boys could speak with and who could translate for Katherine and John.

Lin, John Jr., David, and Mary were an eager welcoming party for Vorin and Pitou. Pitou, age six, greeted them with a warm smile. But Vorin, a tall, skinny eleven-year-old, gave them a piercing, angry stare. The first few days were quiet. Both boys were exhausted and needed to get used to what seemed like a whole new world.

One day Katherine found Vorin screaming, kicking, and having a full-blown tantrum. The other children watched, wide-eyed. Katherine used all of her strength to calm him. Even then, she wasn't completely successful. Vorin was strong and outraged.

"What on earth happened?" Katherine finally asked.

"Gee, Mom, I'm not sure," John Jr. said, looking bewildered. "We were just fooling around and he went berserk."

Katherine called the Cambodian man, who spoke with Vorin. The man told Katherine that Vorin was convinced everyone wanted to kill him, although he assured Vorin this wasn't true. Since events in Cambodia had been so terrifying, Vorin had reason to feel paranoid. A bigger problem, though, was that Vorin was insanely jealous of his brothers, especially Pitou. In Cambodia, Vorin's father had sent him out to sell gasoline on the black market to help make a living for the family, while the younger boys had been allowed to attend school. Vorin had felt deprived and less loved. He was so enraged that he sometimes felt like killing Pitou.

Vorin's rages continued, as did frequent calls to the Cambodian translator. The Patersons sent Vorin to school with the other children; after all, school was what he had wanted. But the teachers reported that Vorin was uncontrollable there, too. He would calm down as long as he had the constant, undivided attention of an adult, but this was impractical for both the school and the Patersons, so he often stayed home.

Before long, social workers called to say that the third brother had been found. Would the Patersons like to take him in as well? No, Katherine said. They had more than they could handle. The brother was welcome to spend time in their home during the day, but they had neither the room nor the energy for another full-time responsibility.

Another family in the area agreed to take the boy. He visited often, coming in the morning and going to school with the other children. He fit in well, and although Vorin didn't like him, Vorin's main rival was Pitou.

Katherine struggled through each day, feeling like a failure. These were children, after all, and she and John were adults. Shouldn't they be able to handle the problems? Why was she flunking?

Lin, John Jr., David, and Mary were equally upset. They hadn't bargained for so much trouble. They had just wanted another brother or sister to pal around with, another one of "them." Maybe, they whispered, we could keep Pitou and get rid of Vorin.

No way, Katherine said. That was all Vorin needed, to be rejected again in favor of Pitou. It wouldn't be fair. Besides, she still believed, now more than ever, that taking in another child wasn't feasible, not permanently.

Pitou and Vorin stayed with the Patersons several months because finding more permanent homes took longer than expected. During that time things improved slightly. Katherine remembered reading that hospital workers sometimes hold disturbed children tightly to calm them, so she tried the approach during one of Vorin's tantrums. She grabbed him around his waist and held on. He flailed but didn't break loose. He was strong enough to free himself if he wanted, so Katherine knew her embrace must somehow be comforting.

Just as Washington's National Zoo had been a treat years ago for her sixth graders in Lovettsville, it once again brought comfort and joy to children in Katherine's care. There was a special open house day for friends of the zoo, and Katherine and John took the whole family, including Vorin and Pitou. As part of the festivities, each child was given a yellow helium balloon.

Before long Katherine saw Vorin let go of his balloon string. It sailed above his head, straight for the sky.

Oh no, she thought. *Here comes a tantrum.* She prepared to lunge into her stronghold.

Instead of screaming, Vorin smiled. Apparently he had let go on purpose. "Yellow balloon!" he shouted gleefully. "Yellow balloon!" For once, his fear and anger were as far away as his homeland. He was just a tall, skinny, eleven-year-old, full of nothing but joy. The moment was short, but incredibly sweet.

Eventually Vorin did change, but the process was

gradual, and didn't happen with the Patersons. All three brothers were placed in more permanent foster homes. Vorin asked to be placed separately from his brothers, and his wish was granted. The two younger boys moved away and their new family didn't keep in touch with the Patersons.

Vorin's new family, the Schlegels, passed along news of Vorin, however, and Vorin remained in contact with his brothers. The Schlegels already had a daughter of their own and two adopted Korean girls, but they very much wanted a son. Mr. Schlegel had been in the military, stationed on the Cambodian border, where he had helped deliver a Cambodian baby born prematurely. He had built an incubator to keep the tiny boy alive. The boy would be about Vorin's age, so the Schlegels felt a special bond with Vorin.

In the end, Vorin adjusted to American life more easily than did his younger brothers. He learned English quickly, was good at sports, and was mechanically gifted. He was old enough to understand that by sending their children away, his parents had saved their lives. He often told his brothers how lucky they were to be in the United States and that they should be thankful and adjust to their new lives.

The Schlegels sent Christmas cards to the Patersons every year. They learned that Vorin joined the army and later became an auto mechanic. In the early 1990s, a miracle happened. Vorin received a letter from his father in Cambodia, who had managed to track him down. Vorin had feared him dead. At last word, they were in touch but hadn't seen each other.

When Vorin and Pitou left the Patersons, Katherine felt guilty. She couldn't get the boys off her mind; she couldn't understand why she hadn't been able to help them more. After all, she'd been able to handle her own children's problems.

That was it, Katherine concluded. She hadn't truly dealt with Vorin and Pitou's problems because she knew she didn't have to. They were just visitors; their problems would leave when they did.

I treated them like Kleenex, Katherine told herself. *Like throwaways—disposable people.* She began thinking about the thousands of foster children, kids who are treated like Kleenex their entire lives.

Katherine had a tradition of writing a Christmas story every year for John to read to his congregation during the Christmas Eve service. That December Katherine wrote a story called "Maggie's Gift" about an old man who takes in two foster children. One story wasn't enough, however. Slowly an entire book took shape.

First came a name, Gilly Hopkins. Katherine had been reading J. R. R. Tolkien's *Lord of the Rings* trilogy, and the name of one of the characters, a queen called Galadriel, stuck in her mind. To Katherine, the name was magic. She added the last name Hopkins, later realizing she was unconsciously thinking of the British writer Gerard Manley Hopkins, one of her favorite poets.

After writing "Maggie's Gift," she realized who Gilly was—a foster child born to a young mother who named her Galadriel after reading Tolkien. Gilly's mother wasn't mature enough to take care of her baby, so Gilly is passed along from foster home to foster home.

What kind of a girl was she? Gilly must be bad, Katherine decided, a child nearly impossible to love, not a sugar-sweet child anyone would be happy to take in. So she made Gilly smart and resourceful, yet a liar, a cheat, a thief, and a bigot who curses and swears.

As Katherine explains to those who criticize Gilly, "I am not, in *Gilly*, trying to tell anyone how I think children *ought* to behave. I am trying to tell the story of a lost child who is angry with a world that regards her as disposable and who is fighting it with every available weapon—fair or foul."

In contrast, she made Gilly's foster mother, Maime Trotter, a worthy opponent, just as good as Gilly is bad.

"Trotter," Katherine explains, "is the foster mother I wasn't. I gave Gilly the best foster mother I could possibly imagine."

Chapter 15
Jacob Have I Wrestled

At one point, near desperation, I said to Virginia Buckley: "If I ever finish this book, Virginia, I'm going to mail it to your home address in a plain brown wrapper. And you must promise me that if it is no good, you will not only refuse to publish it, but that you will never tell another soul that it exists."

Newbery Medal acceptance speech
for *Jacob Have I Loved*, June 1981

When did Katherine feel sure she was a writer?

"I'm not even sure yet," she says.

No matter how many books she publishes or how many awards she receives, writing first drafts is always a painful process filled with self-doubt.

"I have no idea when I'm writing a book if it's any good," she confesses, "or if anybody will want to read it. I only hope that when it's done, it won't disgrace my publisher and that children will read it. There is never any guarantee, and I have yet to stumble upon a formula for either. 'To thine own self be true' is about the only motto that I could offer."

In the fall of 1977, for example, Katherine started working on a story that would eventually become *Jacob Have I Loved*. She couldn't figure out what story she wanted to tell and was having so much trouble that whenever friends asked about her work, she growled and grumbled.

"I can't write anymore," she finally complained to John. "I might as well give up."

John listened calmly, barely lifting an eyebrow. "Oh," he replied. "You've reached *that* stage again." Whenever Katherine writes a book, she and John have this discussion at least once, sometimes more.

This much she knew: she wanted to write about siblings, since childhood jealousies plague many people, even into adulthood. She'd certainly had her own problems with sibling rivalry, but told herself she wasn't specifically thinking about her own family. Instead, she thought of the classic battles between brothers and sisters in the Bible—Cain and Abel, Jacob and Esau, Rachel and Leah.

Like an explorer taking the first steps of an expedition, she began to type, trying to find her way. Here is an excerpt from her notes:

> *Her name is Rachel Ellison but I don't know yet where she lives. It might be in the city or in the country. It might even be Japan. It seems important to know what her parents do. How*

does religion come into the story? Will Rachel be burdened by guilt as well as everything else? Will her relationship to God play counterpoint to her relationship with her brother? I said brother, but perhaps after all it has to be a sister. I'm avoiding sister because it comes too close to home. Am I contemplating a book I can't write? The feelings start boiling up every time I begin to think about it. All raw feeling. No story. There has to be a story. There has to be a setting. There has to be something more than boiling anger. Why am I angry? . . . Where is the key that turns this into a book?

Katherine spent days researching Southeast Asian orphans, thinking they might somehow become characters in the story. They didn't.

Ironically, it was Katherine's sister, Helen, who provided the key. For Christmas, Helen gave John Jr. a book called *Beautiful Swimmers: Watermen, Crabs and the Chesapeake Bay.* As soon as Katherine read the intriguing narrative, she realized she had her setting: an island in the bay, home to a lonely 14-year-old girl. Rachel Ellison became Louise Bradshaw of Rass Island, an imaginary place based on real islands of the Chesapeake. Katherine wasn't sure why she had chosen the name, but there it was. She began reading all the books she could find about the bay, which, from her home in Takoma Park, Maryland, was less than an hour away.

The book was finally taking form, though barely. She

took research notes on stacks of index cards, jotting down ideas such as:

> *Old man gets off ferry. He left thirty years before and has come back. Takes shack at farthest end of island to live as recluse.*

> *cats around garbage dump scavenging. Big cats.*

However, real-life events interrupted her work like the hurricanes that blow through the Chesapeake, bringing both triumph and despair. In January 1978 she received word that *Bridge to Terabithia* had won the Newbery Medal. A year later Gilly won a Newbery Honor and a National Book Award (Katherine's second). While cause for great celebration, receiving the awards made life hectic—she had to travel and give speeches and interviews.

Even more disruptive was another family move at the beginning of 1979. After thirteen years of living in Maryland, John took a job with a Presbyterian church in Norfolk, Virginia. Katherine had never lived in one place for as long as she had lived in Maryland, and she hated to leave her friends there. The move was traumatic enough, but worse was the news that Katherine's mother had been diagnosed with cancer. For several weeks Katherine drove back and forth between their new home in Norfolk and her parents' home in Winchester, trying to settle the family in their new home and visiting her mother until her death in late February.

Katherine's world seemed to have turned upside down. She had little time for writing and *Jacob Have I Loved* progressed slowly. Deep down, though, she knew the problems with the book were internal, not due to her grief or the move. Every time she sat down to type, her stomach churned with anxiety. The story was difficult because it meant a great deal to her, reminding her of her own jealous feelings toward her siblings.

The book itself behaved like a belligerent teenager, refusing to obey its creator. For instance, Katherine disliked using first-person narrators, believing they offer too narrow a perspective. Louise Bradshaw's character, however, insisted on telling her own story in her own voice, against Katherine's better judgment. Indeed, her limited perspective turned out to be vital, because at the core of the novel is Louise's blindness to the love and affection offered by her family and friends.

Katherine kept plugging away, churning out new ideas and revisions. She later joked that the only reason she managed to complete the book was that she would regularly lose all her notes, and thus was forced to abandon some of her many ideas.

Finally, John rescued her by suggesting she send the manuscript to Virginia Buckley. He feared she might work on it forever, never finishing.

Virginia called two days after receiving the manuscript. "I love it," she said.

As always, revisions were needed, some of them major. Unlike the laborious task of writing a first draft, however, Katherine describes a productive morning of revising as "bliss."

After several years of wrestling with Louise Bradshaw's story, Katherine finally had a book. *Jacob Have I Loved* was published in 1980, and in 1981, Katherine found herself on a podium, once again accepting a Newbery Medal. She began her acceptance speech by saying she was "thrilled, honored, gratified, not to say shocked" when she heard she had won.

Every book, no matter how highly praised and honored, has its critics. Some reviewers complained about the ending of *Jacob*—that events happen too quickly, that Louise is a poor "role model," that she makes "poor choices" in love and vocation. Such criticism always hurts. Sometimes Katherine feels like yelling. She cares for her characters deeply, like good friends or family.

In the end, the reactions of young readers, not book critics, are what matter most. Katherine was particularly pleased by a seventh grader who lingered behind her classmates, waiting for a chance to whisper: "I loved *Jacob Have I Loved*."

Moments like that send Katherine's spirits soaring. "No writer could ask for more," she says.

Afterward

Since 1986 Katherine and John have lived in Barre, Vermont, where John was pastor of a Presbyterian church until he retired in 1995. After wandering so much of her life, Katherine hopes never to leave Barre, but cautions, "The way life is, one can never be sure of anything like that."

The children are grown. Lin is a social worker who helps mentally disadvantaged adults. Her husband, Stephen Pierce, is a high school English teacher and volleyball coach. They have two daughters: Katherine, six, and Margaret, three. Their parents read to them often; young Katherine heard *Lyddie*, which was dedicated to her father, at least twice before she was a year old. Katherine's namesake says she wants to write and illustrate books when she grows up.

John Jr. works in marketing for Time Warner, Inc. His wife, Samantha Loomis Paterson, works for American Express *Departures* magazine.

David is an actor, playwright, and carpenter. He wrote a musical adaptation of *The Great Gilly Hopkins* for the stage, which premiered in the fall of 1996 in Louisville, Kentucky, at Stage One, the oldest professional children's theater in the United States. Katherine has seen the show three times and proclaims it "wonderful." David's wife, Ariana Tadler Paterson, is a lawyer in New York City. They expect their first child in the spring of 1997.

Mary is the coordinator of the Race and Cultural Relations Program at the University of Vermont. Mary, John Jr., and Stephen write, although none has tried to be published. Mary has kept voluminous journals since the age of eight.

Katherine stays busy writing, but now that the children are grown, she has more spare time for reading, quilting, doing crossword puzzles, playing Scrabble and tennis, going to the movies, and watching television. She adores music, plays the piano (badly, she says), and sings in the church choir.

John collects art. To display his collection, he built a gallery in the loft of a small barn connected to their home. The Patersons named the gallery "Minna Murra," the Australian aboriginal way of saying, "a quiet, secluded place."

Katherine has her own secluded getaway: an upstairs study built into the eaves of their home, away from the telephone, the doorbell, and the comings and goings of family and friends. She has chosen several works of Japanese art for her walls, including a print called *Big Wave* by a famous artist named Hokusai. She also has an original work by another revered Japanese artist, Kuwabara Totaro, whom she once met. He was Christian, and Katherine owns one of his representations of the loaves and fishes parable, in which Jesus miraculously provides food for a crowd.

Art isn't the only inspiration near her desk. She sometimes looks at an index card on which she copied a Greek saying in large letters:

BEFORE THE GATES OF EXCELLENCE
THE HIGH GODS HAVE PLACED SWEAT.

A *Peanuts* cartoon says much the same thing: Snoopy paces in front of his typewriter and observes, "Good writing is hard work."

Katherine thrives on this Greco-Snoopy philosophy, pouring herself into every character she creates. As she explains in an essay called "The Perilous Realm of Realism":

> *I don't seem to have ever created a character that some corner of my soul does not personally claim— from the rogue samurai Takanobu to Monster Mouth Myers. I am all of them—the wily Saburo as well as the fearful Jesse. A character may be a confession of secret sin or a revelation of hidden longings, but my fantasies are as much me as is my public face, and all my characters are as true, therefore, to the facts of my life as I have the skill to make them.*

As you can see, Katherine is all of her characters, and yet none of them—she is her own self. Young readers are always asking whether the stories in her books really happened. Instead of explaining that her novels are fiction, Katherine Paterson responds: "I hope so. I meant for them to be true. I tried hard to make them so."

Truer words were never spoken.

Time Line

1932   Katherine Clements Womeldorf is born in Qingjiang, China, on October 31.

1938   The Womeldorfs evacuate China; Katherine visits the United States for the first time.

1939   The Womeldorfs return to China.

1940   Once again, war forces the family to evacuate China.

1941   Katherine begins the fourth grade in Winston-Salem, North Carolina.

1946   The Womeldorfs move to Richmond, Virginia.

1950   Katherine graduates from high school in Charles Town, West Virginia, and enters King College in Tennessee, where she majors in English.

1954   Katherine graduates from King College and teaches sixth grade in Lovettsville, Virginia.

1957   After earning a master's degree at the Presbyterian School of Christian Education in Richmond, Virginia, Katherine begins four years of missionary work in Japan.

1961   Katherine returns to the United States and earns another master's degree at Union Theological Seminary in New York.

1962	On July 14 Katherine marries John Barstow Paterson.
1963–64	Katherine teaches at Pennington School for Boys in New Jersey. John Jr. is born and daughter, Lin, is adopted.
1966	Son, David, is born.
1968	Daughter, Mary, is adopted.
1973	Katherine publishes her first novel, *The Sign of the Chrysanthemum*.
1977	*The Master Puppeteer* receives a National Book Award.
1978	*Bridge to Terabithia* receives the Newbery Medal.
1979	*The Great Gilly Hopkins* receives a National Book Award. The Patersons move from Takoma Park, Maryland, to Norfolk, Virginia.
1981	*Jacob Have I Loved* receives the Newbery Medal.
1986	Katherine and John move from Norfolk to Barre, Vermont.
1995	John retires from the ministry. Katherine continues to write from their Vermont home.

Books by Katherine Paterson

Who Am I?, 1966

The Sign of the Chrysanthemum, 1973

Of Nightingales That Weep, 1974

The Master Puppeteer, 1976

Bridge to Terabithia, 1977

The Great Gilly Hopkins, 1978

Angels and Other Strangers: Family Christmas Stories, 1979

Jacob Have I Loved, 1980

The Crane Wife (picture book, Katherine translated story), 1981

Gates of Excellence: On Reading and Writing Books for Children, 1981

Rebels of the Heavenly Kingdom, 1983

Come Sing, Jimmy Jo, 1985

Consider the Lilies: Flowers of the Bible (with John Paterson), 1986

The Tongue-Cut Sparrow (picture book, Katherine translated story), 1987

Park's Quest, 1988

The Spying Heart: More Thoughts on Reading and Writing Books for Children, 1989

The Tale of the Mandarin Ducks (picture book), 1990

Lyddie, 1991

The Smallest Cow in the World (beginning reader), 1991

The King's Equal (beginning reader), 1992

Flip-Flop Girl, 1994

A Midnight Clear: Stories for the Christmas Season, 1995

A Sense of Wonder: On Reading and Writing Books for Children (a one-volume collection of essays including *Gates of Excellence* and *The Spying Heart*), 1995

The Angel and the Donkey (picture book), 1996

Jip: His Story, 1996

About the Author

Alice Cary has worked as a freelance writer and editor for several years, and previously as the managing editor of a weekly newspaper in Massachusetts. Her articles and photographs have appeared in *The Boston Globe*, *Boston Magazine*, *TV Guide*, *USA Today*, and *Sports Illustrated for Kids*. She regularly reviews children's books for *Book Page*. She is also the author of *Jean Craighead George*, another book in The Learning Works *Meet the Author* series.

Alice lives in Groton, Massachusetts, with her husband and their young son.